Soviet Attack Submarines

~

Cold War Operations and Accidents

Soviet Attack Submarines

~

Cold War Operations
and Accidents

By
Mark H. Glissmeyer

Gradina Books

Today the Russian submarine fleet has developed to where some of their submarine classes can enter foreign waters almost undetected to operate at will, however that wasn't always the case. The early development actually happened during the Cold War years of the Soviet Union, at the cost of many injuries and untold lives. From those early beginnings until later having stealth technologies, it was always a goal to operate at such a sophisticated level that a submarine could become truly "invisible". This is the story of how it was made possible. This Cold War book is based on recently released CIA documents concerning the development of the Soviet submarine fleet. Information in this book is based on recently declassified documents sourced and derived from the Central Intelligence Agency (CIA).

Copyright © 2023 by Mark H. Glissmeyer

All rights reserved.

No part of this book may be reproduced, or stored in a retrieval system, or transmitted in any form or by any means, electronic, mechanical, recording, photocopying or otherwise, without the express written permission of the publisher. This book is not endorsed by any of the governmental agencies, newspapers, periodicals, military divisions, or related individuals mentioned.

Gradina Books

ISBN-13: 979-8-9855771-2-9

Other maritime titles by this author:

MV Hughes Glomar Explorer: The Top Secret Mission

Maritime Academy Graduate: Memoir Of A Third Mate

Dedication:

During the Cold War, the Soviet Navy experienced over sixteen major accidents involving their submarines at sea, resulting in the loss of more than 588 crewmembers. While they were an adversary to the United States, many of their stories are a testament to their bravery. This book is dedicated in their memory.

Table Of Contents:

Evolution of the Soviet Submarine Force: 2
The Start Of The Cold War: 3
The Growth of Interdiction Forces: 6
First Soviet Cold War Attack Classes: 9
The Atom Bomb 1945: 14
Early Submarine Design Dangers: 22
Ballistic-Missile Submarine Program Begins: 23
The Development of Anti-Carrier Capabilities: 29
Advancements With Anti-Ship Torpedoes: 46
More Submarine Casualties: 57
Contending With US Carriers: 63
The Development of Anti-Submarine Capabilities: 71
Scope of Distant Submarine Operations: 86
Soviet Capabilities for Submarine Detection: 110
A Stolen Submarine: 118
The Modernization Of Soviet Submarines: 121
Modern Soviet War Strategy: 124
Soviet Leadership Changes: 146
A Secret Accident: 152
1990 Final Judgments: 166
The Soviet Submarine Legacy: 172

Introduction:

Following the unimpressive performance of the Soviet Navy during World War Two, Soviet leadership realized that a stronger navy would be an important factor in their drive to gain recognition for their world power status. In less than a decade, the Soviet Union would develop a large naval force and would operate the largest submarine fleet in the world. By Stalin's death in 1953, their naval development program was well advanced; nine cruisers had been completed, construction had begun on two of a programmed four heavy cruisers, and construction of aircraft carriers was reportedly planned. The Soviet Navy was becoming a force which might eventually attempt to contest control of the high seas from the United States, as well as defend the USSR against any seaborne attack.

This book traces the history and missions of the Soviet attack submarine force and describes the various classes of attack submarines which the Soviets built. It also discusses Soviet naval operations such as the conscription of their crews, and includes various submarine accidents at sea. It gives this chronology from two different viewpoints—that of the United States gleamed through US intelligence, and also from the viewpoint of the Soviet military. *The viewpoint of the Soviet military is given in italics.*

The following United States Navy hull classifications are used in this book for describing submarines:

SS–the SS for subsurface denotes submarine
SSB–the added B denotes ballistic missile submarine
SSG–the added G denotes guided missile submarine
SSN–the added N denotes nuclear-powered submarine
SSBN–denotes ballistic missile nuclear-powered submarine
SSGN–denotes guided missile nuclear-powered submarine

Evolution of the Soviet Submarine Force:

The Soviet Union entered World War Two with approximately 160 submarines having various combat strengths, but due to their inferior performance the Soviets were determined to improve their abilities using captured assets. It was common knowledge that the Germans had created in the Type XXI combat U-boat, from designs developed by Professor Hellmuth Walter, a submarine capable of remaining underwater for longer periods and thereby evading any radar detection (with radar only being effective above the ocean's surface). Of great importance during the war was the fact that the assembly yard at Gdynia, Poland housed the latest German submarine in development and fell into the hands of the Soviet troops. Somehow, the capture of this production facility was carefully kept a secret even from the Allies, and was so important that the Soviet Navy later concentrated the bulk of their naval construction program on the development and construction of these "Elektroboot" submarines.

A German submarine design group had also worked in Germany at Blankenburg (Harz). This German group worked first with the type XXI submarine, and later on the type XXVI submarine design. The group also worked on the Walter engine for the latter. When the Soviets entered Blankenburg in 1945, they found and conscripted from this program the two lead German scientists who began working for them. These two scientists then divulged other specialists who were still in Blankenburg, and the Soviets recruited these and others who were brought in for this special design bureau. In September of 1946, the bureau began working on the re-construction of the type XXVI submarine. Three to four months later, a Soviet Navy colonel arrived and took over leadership of the group. The group was then given the main interest directed at reproducing the propulsion system (eventually being commissioned as the Soviet Whiskey class submarine).

The Soviet naval staff operating in Germany also showed strong interest in searching for evidence of German submarine tests using secret V-weapons. Since Germany had fired rockets with low initial velocities from submarines and had reached a fairly advanced stage through experiments, the Soviets were keen on continuing this progress through the further development of the V-weapons program. Meanwhile, construction using older Soviet submarine designs continued, and a few years later in 1949 the USSR had amassed around 250 submarines within their fleet, which included 100 captured German units and approximately 150 newer submarines built since 1945. Later on, starting in 1950, a more modern Soviet attack submarine force began development that would encompass four general phases during the Cold War. (See Figure 1 on page 5 showing the chronology of the first three phases from 1950 to 1975.)

The Start Of The Cold War:

So when did the Cold War really begin? In many western countries it is generally agreed that the Cold War started after World War Two in 1947, since this is when the Truman Doctrine was announced as a means to limit our Soviet sphere of influence. However, the actual start of this period might also be pinpointed to the Yalta Conference held in early February of 1945. At the time fighting in World War Two was still in the advancement period towards Berlin within Nazi Germany, while the eventual Axis defeat was already considered a certainty. The three major Allied world leaders–Roosevelt, Churchill, and Stalin–met to discuss what Europe would become in the post war period, and how this territory was to be divided up amongst these world powers. It was decided that Berlin would be split into three parts, with each part being controlled by a separate power, and a fourth part being split out for France. The outcome for Poland was promises were made by us for free elections, but our Soviet government would control the country post war. This was a major victory for Stalin, as it eventually gave our country influence all the way from Moscow to Berlin, and set up the Cold War for years to come.

One other important note about this time is that some in the American military already knew what U.S. political leaders apparently refused to believe. It was how the real conflict was to become this East/West standoff, arguing that with all of the surviving Allied military equipment in Europe still at the ready, maybe this future conflict would be better off if it was settled right after Germany surrenders. The American General Patton was one who vocalized this to his superiors, and was quickly relieved of command as a result when cooler heads prevailed back in Washington. But it wasn't that long before the first real test for our country against the West started, and it happened when the Japanese unconditionally surrendered in the Pacific. The Chinese Civil War that had been stalemated as a result of the Pacific Conflict started back up, and both the West and our country took opposing sides. The ink was barely dry on the Japanese surrender when weapons were being funneled through, and we helped our communist brothers to slowly, but relentlessly, defeat the Nationalist Party until they retreated back to Taiwan in 1949. America had lost their first major proxy war during the Cold War era within four years, and it wouldn't be the last.

Another interesting proxy war that seems forgotten was how the Korean peninsula came to be divided. The division actually happened with the surrender of the Japanese at the end of World War Two, where it was proposed by American leaders that two occupation zones should be created after the Japanese withdrawal.

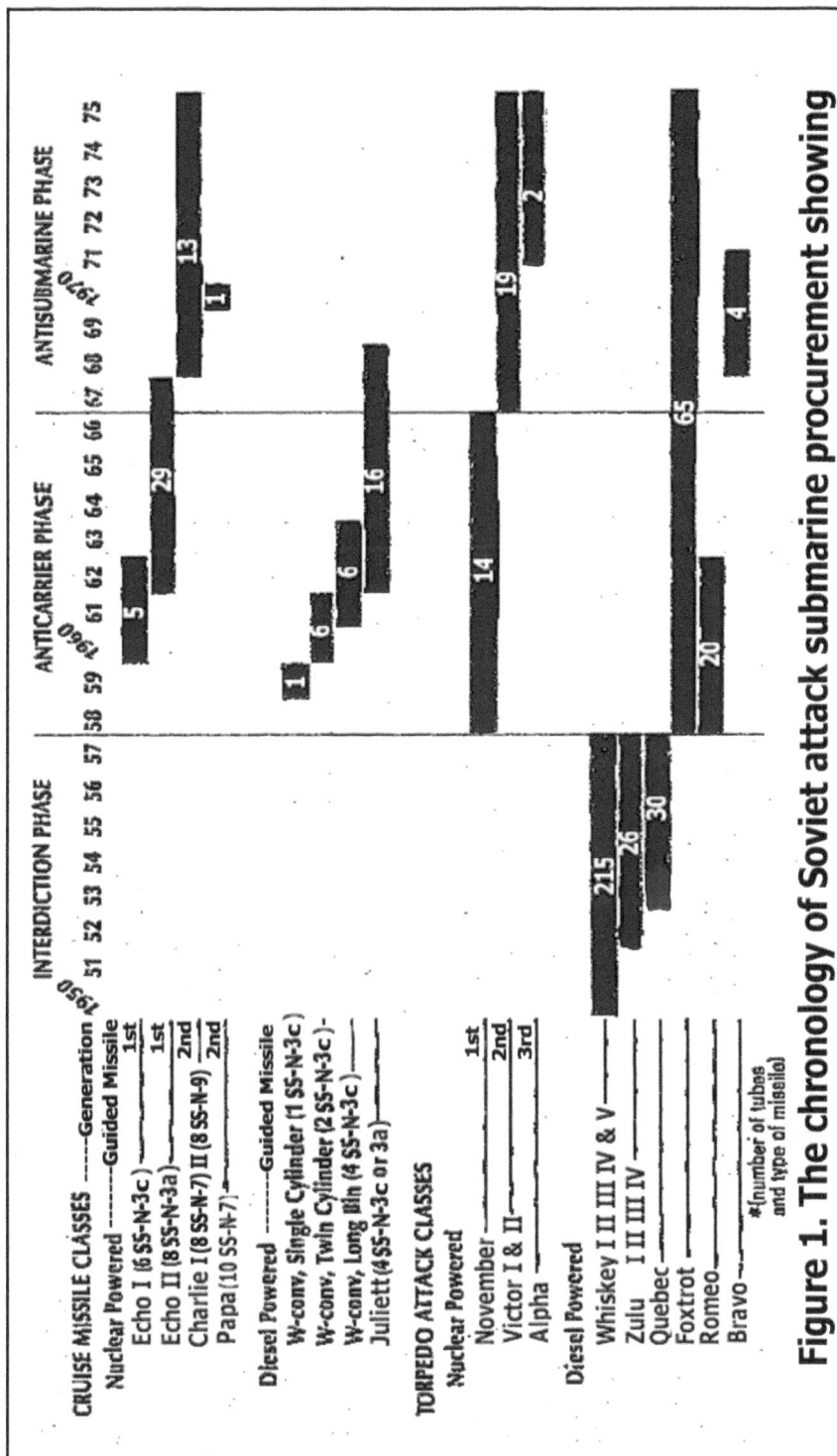

Figure 1. The chronology of Soviet attack submarine procurement showing the interdiction, anti-carrier and anti-submarine phases from 1950 to 1975.

One would be a southern zone that they would control up to the 38th parallel, and the northern half would be controlled by us. This was readily accepted by our Soviet leadership and implemented by both sides after the war. The inevitable stalemate in negotiations for the future of Korea lasted for years, until a war began between both Korean sides after governmental elections were finally held. With the north invading the south in 1950, this was a new proxy war that our side was determined to win. That year 1950 was also an important year because it was really the dawn to the start of our new submarine age. With our Soviet nuclear weapons being developed and nuclear power designs also becoming a possibility, our fleet was to eventually transform into a modern era that competed against the imperialistic West. In simple terms, we had our proxy wars on land, and the Cold War was also to be carried out under the oceans.

1950-1957 Phase
The Growth of Interdiction Forces:

After the Second World War had ended, the Soviets recognized that the outcome of a future war with the West might depend on their ability to disrupt or sever the US supply routes to Europe, and to defend the sea approaches to the USSR. Impressed with the success of German interdiction efforts during World War Two, Stalin decided on a massive submarine procurement program as his solution to this problem of interdiction—possibly as many as one-thousand new submarines were planned to be built. The Soviets also studied German construction methods and designs and used expatriated Germans to work on the program.

Shortly after Nikita Khrushchev was elected Soviet leader after Stalin's death in 1953, the changes brought about by the advent of atomic power started to cause doubts about the fundamental assumptions on which their naval building program had earlier been based. Soviet leaders recognized that their plan to wage an active contest for control of the seas was unrealistic. Nuclear warfare had created an entirely new situation in which submarines could serve as strategic weapons, and small, missile-equipped surface ships could become the equal of much larger conventionally armed vessels. In such a strategy, quality could count for as much as quantity. Although the Soviet Navy would retain its traditional missions of interdicting the enemy's sea communications, defending the coasts of the USSR, and supporting the seaward flanks of the Red Army, its basic mission was to be expanded. This included planning for the strategic defense of the USSR against seaborne nuclear attack, and the launching of missile attacks against enemy territory.

This was established in 1955 when Khrushchev made statements that submarines with guided missiles were to become the preferable naval weapons used by his country, and their development would become emphasized by the Soviet Navy. His vision was for many of the Soviet long-range submarines to be equipped to carry one or two cruise missiles using topside stowage, and as an interim measure, the USSR would equip them in much the same manner as those of the US Navy–by using storage housing and launch ramps on deck. Not surprisingly, US intelligence reports from widely-separated areas began describing Soviet submarines with suspicious-looking topside installations on them about a year later. At this same time it was observed that the construction of new cruisers had ceased, and it seemed apparent to Western observers that no Soviet carriers were ever going to be built.

US intelligence also observed another significant change in the Soviet submarine program, when their sub construction declined sharply with the completion of the

Whiskey and Quebec classes in 1957. This occurred after the construction of a record eighty-three submarines in 1956–more than any other nation had ever built in a single year. While the construction of conventional submarines was being sharply curtailed, a shift to the construction of new submarine types was begun. These new concepts also were reflected with the introduction of new ships, armament, and propulsion plants. These were eventually to include conventional and nuclear-powered submarines equipped with ballistic or cruise type surface-to-surface missiles, gas turbine propulsion systems, new torpedoes and anti-submarine weapons, and surface ships equipped with surface-to-surface and surface-to-air missiles.

This development happened during a postwar building program unprecedented in peacetime history, since by mid-1957 the USSR had built their submarine force to number approximately 450 boats. This strength, incidentally, was nearly eight times the submarine strength with which Germany had entered World War II, and was greater than Germany's peak submarine strength in May of 1943. About 240, or a little more than half, of the Soviet submarines at the time were mostly medium range units using postwar designs and construction methods. Nevertheless, in 1957 the Soviets stopped far short of their goal of one-thousand submarines. In total, 271 submarines of the post-war Whiskey, Zulu, and Quebec classes were built for the Soviet Union, fewer than a third of those originally planned.

From 1958 to 1966, the focus of their efforts shifted to the development of a force of cruise missile submarines to cope with the threat of US aircraft carriers. Later, a third shift in emphasis became apparent in 1967 when they introduced the first in a series of attack submarines designed for anti-submarine warfare (ASW), which was a natural response to the large Polaris submarine force which the United States was developing during the early 1960s. The final phase started in 1976 which was to modernize their entire Soviet submarine fleet.

First Soviet Cold War Attack Classes: 1950 Whiskey Class

The Whiskey class SS (*Project 613*) was designed as an improvement over the earlier Srednyaya class Soviet attack submarines—nicknamed *Stalinets* by Soviet submariners—which were used during World War Two, including the incorporated aspects of German U-Boat design, and they entered service starting in 1950. (See Figure 2.) Their submerged speed was only 13 knots, while they had a length of 249 feet. Their operating depth limit was 656 feet. These were diesel electric submarines that only compared in size to the SS-205 submarine built in 1941 by the United States. The Whiskey class became the most numerous submarine of any class within the Soviet fleet during this phase, eventually comprising nearly eighty percent of the entire Soviet submarine fleet. There were five different variations of the Whiskey class submarine that entered service.

- Whiskey-I had twin 25mm guns mounted into the conning tower.
- Whiskey-II had twin 25mm and twin 57mm guns.
- Whiskey-III had their guns removed.
- Whiskey-IV had 25mm guns and was fitted with a snorkel.
- Whiskey-V had no guns and a streamlined conning tower with a snorkel.

The Whiskey class was intended as a medium range submarine meant mainly for coastal defenses, and as an antiship weapon. Only the later versions were given a snorkel, which was a mast that allowed for continuous diesel operations and battery charging while submerged near the surface. They had for armament 21-inch torpedo tubes, with four at the bow, and two at the stern. Each unit carried up to twelve torpedoes, and had a crew of fifty-two. Some later boats were converted to cruise missile submarines starting in 1959, and a further sixty were eventually upgraded to be Whiskey-V versions. The Whiskey class was considered to be a major improvement over earlier World War Two era Soviet submarines, but they also had some limitations. Two issues that needed improvement was the noise level they created while operating, as well as the slow speed of their propulsion system. Diesel electrics were known to be relatively slow underwater, yet faster while on the surface. It was only when nuclear propulsion arrived in the later submarine classes that this speed differential was finally reversed.

1952 Zulu Class

Another of the first post-World War Two attack submarines produced by the Soviet Union was the Zulu class SS (*Project 611*). The Zulu class was also based on German U-Boat design, and were in development at the same time as the Whiskey class. (See Figure 3.) They started entering service in 1952 and had a submerged speed of 16 knots. They included an overall length of 295 feet, and had an operating depth limit of 750 feet. These were also diesel electric and had six 21-inch torpedo tubes at the bow, with four at the stern. They could carry up to twenty-two torpedoes each. Five different versions were eventually in service, with the major upgrade being for six units carrying ballistic missiles starting in 1956. The Zulu class was a larger submarine than the Whiskey class, and were designed for having longer patrols away from the Soviet coastline. Twenty-six Zulu submarines eventually entered service, and each carried a crew of seventy-two.

Figure 2. The procurement program for the medium range Whiskey class diesel-powered submarine was the largest ever undertaken by the Soviets.

Figure 3. The Zulu class diesel-powered submarine was the first Soviet long range attack submarine. A conversion of this class from 1955 to 1957 resulted in the first Soviet ballistic missile submarine.

1953 Quebec Class

The Quebec class SS (*Project 615*) was designed as a small coastal submarine which included a closed-cycle diesel engine that allowed them to stay underwater for longer durations. (See Figure 4.) The first units entered service in 1953, and each had a submerged speed of 16 knots. With an overall length of 185 feet, they were the smallest of the newer post-World War Two designed Soviet submarines, but due to their use of liquid oxygen, these versions were plagued with safety issues and accidents. Unlike the Zulu class which had three diesel engines, or the Whiskey class which had two, the Quebec class instead used a single closed-cycle diesel engine for its main propulsion, but had two smaller diesels to assist as afterburners. For armament they had four 21-inch torpedo tubes at the bow, with room to carry four torpedoes. They had an operating depth limit of 400 feet. Thirty units entered service from 1952 to 1958, and each carried a crew of twenty-nine.

Soviet Attack Submarine Operations:

The medium and short-range Whiskey and Quebec class submarines, while operating from the Northern Fleet, could not be used effectively against US sea lines of communication to Europe since they were some 1,800 to 2,400 nm distant. The Whiskey class submarines, under optimum conditions, could remain on a patrol station at that distance from its base for only about ten days. They were therefore better suited to defending the sea approaches to the USSR, and to interdict any US naval vessels operating in the Norwegian Sea. Of the submarines built during this phase, only the few long-range Zulu class units were suitable for reaching the US shipping lines to Europe and conducting lengthy patrol operations.

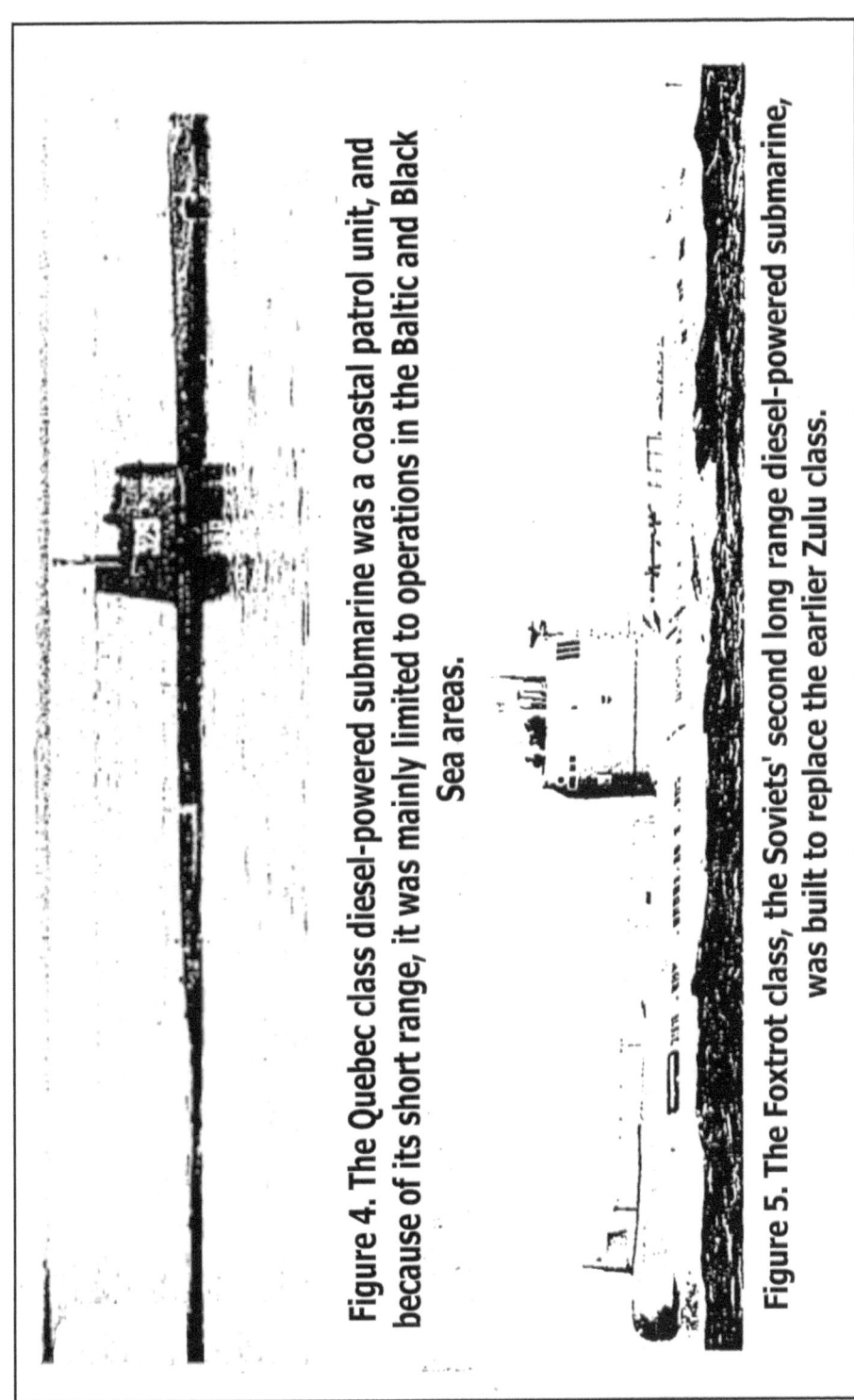

Figure 4. The Quebec class diesel-powered submarine was a coastal patrol unit, and because of its short range, it was mainly limited to operations in the Baltic and Black Sea areas.

Figure 5. The Foxtrot class, the Soviets' second long range diesel-powered submarine, was built to replace the earlier Zulu class.

Eventually, the development of nuclear-powered submarines in the US hastened the end of the large Zulu, Whiskey, and Quebec class procurement programs. The Soviets were aware of the capabilities of nuclear submarines, and were proceeding with the development of the November class which was capable of operating twenty days on station with a 5,800 nm patrol radius, or thirty days at 4,300 nm. The Soviets also continued to improve their sea line interdiction capability, but in the late 1950s a more serious threat was recognized–the US aircraft carriers and their potential for nuclear strikes on the Soviet Union. To meet the carrier threat, the Soviets later developed cruise missile submarines that were capable of striking a US carrier before any of its attacking aircraft could be launched.

The Atom Bomb 1945:

Many may wonder how our country actually acquired the knowledge to develop nuclear power and nuclear weapons so quickly. It actually began shortly after the Americans successfully dropped atom bombs on the Japanese cities of Hiroshima and Nagasaki at the end of World War Two, where for a while they boasted of being the only nuclear power on the planet. And while this might have seemed it gave them a guaranteed military superiority over the rest of the world, it must be remembered that their atom bomb design had to be released from inside a flying aircraft, which meant it had a limited range it could be used, and that was assuming it made it past defending air defenses.

Our country knew of the possibilities of nuclear weapons starting in the late 1930's, with a Soviet proposal finally initiated in 1940 to begin nuclear planning. However, this was not advanced until after the Nazis invaded our motherland, and Stalin gave the order to begin intelligence gathering in 1942 towards a realistic nuclear program. When our country was advancing to Berlin in the late stages of the war, we had a contest amongst our own armies—with two of them racing to win control of Berlin, motivated by a desire to gain control of the German nuclear research program at the Kaiser Wilhelm Institute before the Americans would arrive.

We also knew of the Manhattan Project, and attempted to learn all we could through our clandestine spy network. Then something curious happened, we heard through intelligence that some of the scientists involved in the American project were dismayed at hearing that the ultimate aim of the program was not only meant to end World War Two, but also was for the eventual defeat of our own country as well. This was the crack we needed to actually have a few of the Manhattan Project nuclear scientists work against the US government.

Later after the war in 1946, the Americans did some well publicized nuclear testing out at Bikini Atoll to see how nuclear explosions could sink various ship designs. The results were heralded by the West as confirmation of how this new weapon could win any future war, and their imperialist allies believed it as well. Using all available sources, including those obtained from the German nuclear scientists who came and worked on our side, spurred on by the American tests at Bikini Atoll, we developed our own nuclear program rapidly until on the 29th of August, 1949, we successfully tested our first nuclear device.

It coincidentally looked a lot like the Fat Man design that was successfully dropped on Japan by America, and for good reason. Many of the specifications used were obtained from the Los Alamos research facility using clandestine means. Even procuring the uranium ores and precious metals, then refining them turned out to be a great achievement. If America thought they had total military superiority over us, it hadn't lasted for long.

Problems In The Soviet Submarine Service:

Next to revealing any of their Soviet state secrets, the greatest sin against their navy seemed to be the exposure of deficiencies in their Soviet built and operated equipment. Any faithful reader of the Soviet press after World War Two would hardly be aware that Soviet airplanes ever crashed or that Soviet ships ever got lost at sea. In 1955 when the battleship Novorossisk struck a mine and carried some nine-hundred crewmembers to their deaths, the Soviet public was never informed about the tragedy. However, despite using stringent security measures, news of accidents sometimes still filtered out accidentally. There were several reports of Soviet submarine accidents ranging from fuel explosions to collisions. Some vessels and crews went missing. Some of this could be blamed on ice, fog, and darkness, but much was due to their inadequate personnel training and faulty military equipment designs.

The Dangerous Quebec Class:

One costly design experiment was the Quebec class of torpedo attack submarines which earned them the nickname of *cigarette lighters* amongst Soviet submariners. Of some thirty which were built between 1953 and 1957, the original units had a closed-cycle diesel propulsion system which used liquid oxygen for underwater operations. Although sound in principle, this system was highly explosive unless it was handled with a degree of cleanliness and caution not characteristic of the Soviet Navy. All officers who served on these Quebec boats received a twenty-percent bonus—known as death pay—and each year of their service was credited as eighteen months toward their pay increases and pensions. Other conventional Quebec units had no such built-in problems, but at least one was lost because of faulty navigation. In October of 1956 a collision with a destroyer in the approaches to Tallinn cut her in two, and she sank immediately. Only four seamen escaped the collision, while twenty-seven bodies were recovered from the submarine sections a month later.

Whiskey Submarine Casualties:

Seamanship seems to have been the chief cause of accidents involving the Whiskey class torpedo attack submarines, which were designed and built from well tested components. In 1957 one in the Black Sea ran aground at a depth of two-hundred feet. Fortunately for the crew, a destroyer managed to attach a line and pull the submarine back to the surface. A few cases of carbon dioxide poisoning were the only casualties in that case. However, most of the Whiskey casualties occurred in the Northern Fleet, which had the largest number of submarines while operating under the worst ice and visibility conditions. In 1957 and 1958 two collisions—one with a tug and another with a destroyer—reportedly caused heavy damage to the submarines and killed a number of the sailors.

Design and Damage Control:

Photographs of damaged Soviet submarines often showed that their most vulnerable area was the after section of the sail, from the deck over to the snorkel exhaust. Soviet designers seemingly reduced the cross bracing and the thickness by this area too much in an effort to decrease the weight topside that was critical for strength. Buoyancy characteristics for the Whiskey class submarines were also analyzed, and it was determined that vessels of this class could surface with one of their seven compartments flooded along with one ballast tank. The other Soviet Zulu and Quebec classes of this time period also contained seven watertight compartments, and these too were calculated to be able to surface with one compartment flooded along with one ballast tank. In general, Soviet damage control capabilities were comparable to those of the United States. The Soviets could plug or shore up several small punctures in the pressure hulls of their submarines while operating out at sea. (See Figures 6 and 7 on damage control training.)

Our Soviet Servicemen:

In order to have a disciplined Soviet Navy using crewmembers that would instantly obey any order, we developed extensive regulations which conveyed the importance of our Soviet philosophy, and which applied to those that were within our service. The following military oath governed all of our seamen within the Soviet fleet, and were to be followed without question or hesitation.

A citizen of the Union of Soviet Socialist Republics who entered into the ranks of the Armed Forces took our oath and solemnly swore to be an honest, brave, disciplined and alert serviceman, to strictly preserve military and state secrecy, to observe the USSR Constitution and Soviet laws, and to unquestioningly fulfill all military regulations and orders given by our commanders and superiors. The serviceman also swore to conscientiously study military affairs, protect military and public property in every way, and to remain faithful to our people, the Soviet motherland and to our Soviet state to their last breath alive.

The serviceman was to always be prepared and to rise in the defense of the motherland when ordered to do so by our Soviet government, and as a soldier of the USSR Armed Forces, each swore to protect this courageously, competently, with merit and with honor, neither sparing blood nor life itself in order to achieve total victory over all of our enemies. If any violated this solemn oath of theirs, they would let the severest penalties of our Soviet laws and the universal abhorrence and contempt of our Soviet people fall upon them as punishment.

Soviet Cruise Missile Plans:

In the early 1950s, the Soviet Navy was tasked to protect the coasts of the USSR, and to support the flanks of the Red Army. The Soviet Navy seldom operated more than a few hundred miles from their main coastline. The surface naval forces lacked sufficient armament to operate safely beyond their land-based air cover in the face of Western carrier-borne air power.

The Soviet naval air arm was composed mainly of land-based fighter aircraft and light bombers having short ranges. Only a few of the Soviet's diesel-powered submarines armed with torpedoes ever exercised much beyond their home waters. These were mainly available for the protection of coastal areas, and for interdiction of sea lanes during wartime.

Their attack usefulness against the US carrier was marginal because these Soviet submarines were slow, had a limited submerged range, and had to penetrate the aircraft carrier's large screening forces before they could launch torpedoes against it. Also, the Soviet torpedoes carried aboard their submarines were still unguided versions using World War Two designs. However, they had captured the latest German G7es homing torpedoes at the end of World War Two, and were working to develop a comparable homing system for their own torpedoes, but the first passive homing versions proved to be too unreliable and dangerous at this early stage.

The Soviet Navy in the mid-1950s also wanted to extend their defensive perimeters outward, primarily to counter the nuclear threat of the US carriers. The solution to achieving this was either to construct Soviet aircraft carriers or to develop strike weapons of sufficient range.

Between the two options, the Soviets chose to use cruise missiles as their strike weapon. The available cruise missile technology they developed was acquired from Germany after World War Two. Another benefit with cruise missiles was the lead time to production didn't require the resource base or the research and development timeline of an additional six to eight years compared to developing competing aircraft carriers.

The Soviets had no experience in building or operating carriers, and were already committed to maintaining a costly ship construction program for their coastal defenses. In addition, the Soviets calculated that cruise missiles offered several favorable characteristics which led to lower costs and shorter construction lead times.

Soviet training manuals claimed that cruise missiles had an overall hit probability of from sixty to ninety percent, as compared to under ten percent with naval guns and ten to twenty-five percent for unguided torpedoes. One direct hit with a highly-explosive SS-N-2 Styx missile, according to the manuals, would destroy a transport or a destroyer-size warship. Three hits would destroy a cruiser-size ship. If this textbook ratio was continued, an estimated five to seven hits would be needed to destroy an aircraft carrier, but one hit—in the hangar deck, for example—might prevent the carrier from being able to launch any aircraft altogether. Also of note, cruise missiles were difficult to counter because of the unique flight characteristics which they had. Their speed allowed any US defensive weapons little reaction time. Some missiles in their final approach to a target flew at low altitudes and presented only a small radar return that could be lost in the surface clutter. These characteristics were used during the following few years in planning for Soviet cruise missile conversions within the existing Soviet Whiskey class submarine fleet.

Figure 6. Soviet damage control training showing a leak being blocked off in the pressure hull.

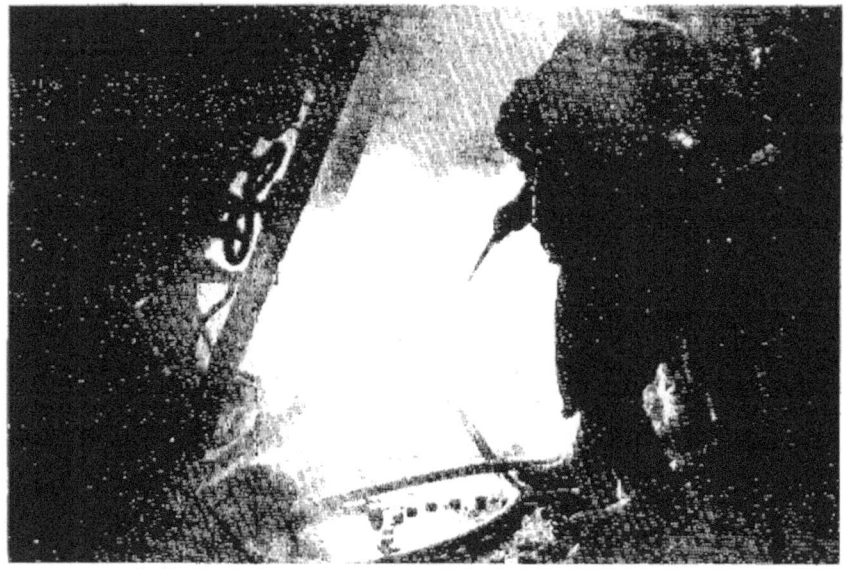

Figure 7. Soviet damage control training showing fire fighting methods being taught for submarines.

Early Submarine Design Dangers:

The many memorials that were built within our Soviet submarine fleet areas were a testament to the bravery and sacrifice that our early submariners gave with their lives. Many of those buried ashore never had their stories told, with some having died by accident, or were recovered years after a submerged death, while others died sacrificing themselves as needed to save fellow crewmembers during an emergency. Early on during the Cold War some submarine designs were created and tested in a hurry, sometimes being the Soviet way to determine if things were possibly feasible and safe. During this time early diesels could not stay submerged for very long, so one submarine was an early Quebec class design that used stored oxygen to feed the diesels so they could remain submerged for longer periods. But this created a dangerous problem, compressed oxygen became an explosive bomb if it was accidentally detonated, since the oxygen itself fed the fire and multiplied the dangers. This is why submarines with this design were often called cigarette lighters by our veteran submariners.

One such accident occurred in the Baltic Sea during 1956, when a small fire started in the engine room compartment with this dangerous design. The crew was able to surface the submarine and they quickly got personnel out onto the main deck for safety, expecting an explosion at any moment as the internal fire grew in size. But as happens sometimes during accidents, what was to be expected didn't come to pass. Instead, in this case the submarine simply sank quickly by the stern, tossing all those out on deck into the stormy seas. Only seven sailors were eventually saved. An official investigation surmised that the sinking was due to the crew not being trained well enough for this advanced engine design, or were simply too lazy to follow safety precautions during underwater operations–this was to become a common way of blaming our seamen when things went wrong.

The Ballistic-Missile Submarine Program Begins:

After Nikita Khrushchev replaced Stalin due to his death in 1953, and Admiral Sergey Gorshkov was appointed by him to be Commander-in-Chief of the Soviet Navy, adjustments appeared in Soviet naval policy which led to later phases of submarine procurement. Of the eleven principal naval shipbuilding programs underway from 1954 to 1955, all but one were shortly phased out and replaced with newer programs such as the Zulu, Golf, and Hotel classes of ballistic-missile submarines, in addition to the Echo-I and modified Whiskey versions of cruise-missile submarines. This was established when construction began for a new diesel-powered Golf class and a nuclear-powered Hotel class at the Severodvinsk Shipyard, along with a diesel-powered Golf class at the Komsomolsk Shipyard in the Soviet Far East. These two classes were the first ones to begin construction specifically for the launching of ballistic missiles, although final construction and fitting out wouldn't be completed until 1958 to 1960. In the meantime, one Zulu-IV and five Zulu-V class (SSB) diesel-powered ballistic-missile submarines were produced from 1956 to 1958, being modified Zulu class (SS) torpedo-attack types that carried either one or two SS-1b Scud missiles. These were the first operational ballistic missile units converted for the Soviet submarine fleet. (See Figure 8 that shows ballistic missile submarine chronology.)

These changes in naval programs were in part a response to a broadening of the Soviet Navy's mission to include the destruction of land targets, and was made possible with the arrival of more lethal long-range weapons. Beginning in

1955, high Soviet officials wrote approvingly of naval missiles that could destroy enemy ships or targets ashore. Khrushchev, for example, stated in April of 1956 that guided-missile submarines were the most suitable naval weapons, and that they would receive emphasis in the future development of the Soviet Navy. The major advantage of using this weapon, Khrushchev asserted, was that it offered the USSR the capability to make defensive attacks on the US directly. However, these early statements were rather vague about the types of shore targets meant to be destroyed. In early 1957, however, industrial and administrative centers in the interior of the United States were identified as suitable targets for naval missile strikes. Putting together such statements with later evidence of corresponding changes in ship construction, the conclusion seems justified that the Soviet Navy was assigned a strategic strike mission starting in 1955.

Concurrently with the gaining of this naval mission came the development of better missile systems. Among the new weapons was the SS-N-3 cruise missile, which was developed primarily for use against ships at sea but could also be employed against enemy coastal targets. Statements by Soviet naval officers, however, indicated that, at least in this early period, ballistic missiles would be favored for strikes against major targets ashore. Accordingly, work on three different ballistic missile designs was undertaken from 1955 to 1959. One of the newest ballistic missiles, a naval variant of the 150-nm-range Scud designated SS-1b (*R-11FM*), was first flight-tested in 1955 and became operational aboard a Zulu-IV class submarine in 1958. A second improved missile, the 350-nm-range SS-N-4 Sark (*R-13*), was still being designed in 1956 and did not enter into flight-testing until mid 1959. A third missile design was being conceived of in 1957. Still, this period saw the firm establishment of a mission to destroy enemy industrial and administrative centers.

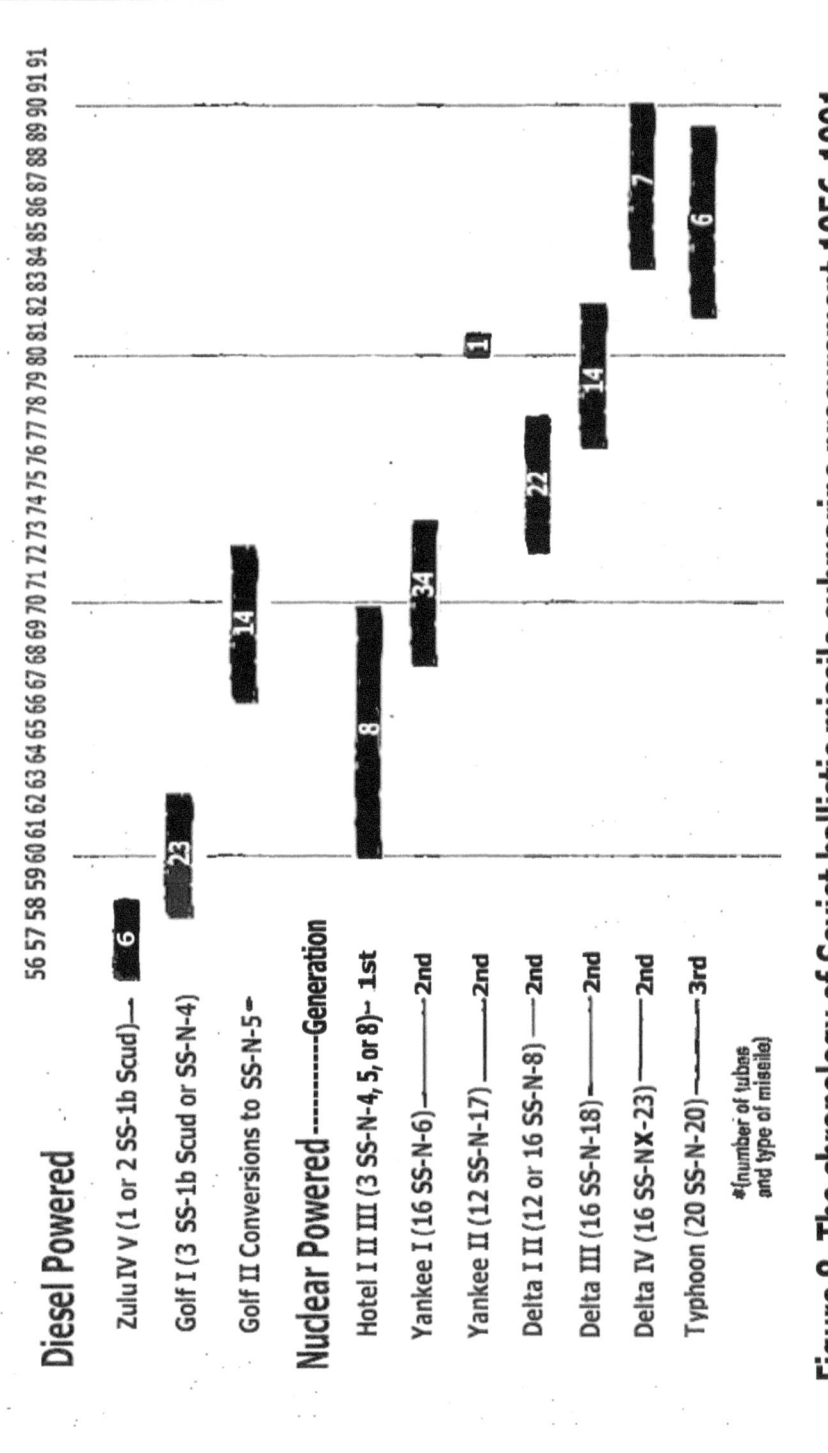

Figure 8. The chronology of Soviet ballistic missile submarine procurement 1956-1991

At the same time, weapons systems were being developed that were intended to carry out that mission using ballistic missiles launched from Soviet submarines.

A Black Sea Accident:

*O*n *one day in 1957, one of our diesel submarines attempted a fast dive during a training exercise while in the Black Sea. In this situation, the commander would normally wait for orders to proceed, then give the dive command after the indicator for the flap valve supplying air to the diesels indicated a closed position. However, the signal to the indicator was faulty and the value wasn't fully closed, leading to heavy flooding in the sixth compartment after the submarine began to submerge. This caused the submarine to start sinking by the stern, and after a seven minute descent, the stern ended up hitting the sandy bottom. But to the horror of the crew, the bow remained up at a sixty degree angle, since the flooded sixth compartment had poured over into the seventh compartment as well. Then a faulty bulkhead and a small fire helped to short out the seventh compartment electrical panels, leading the crew to barely escape forward before stopping the flooding after two exhaustive hours. After analyzing the situation, the commander calculated the sub had forty tons of seawater inside her, with enough air and food to last only two more days for the crew. Also, nobody was sure if the released emergency signal buoy had correctly surfaced. Therefore, the plan for escape was simple, get the seawater out by pumping. So in the old fashioned manner of a fire bucket brigade, the entire crew formed a chain of buckets to pass hand-to-hand the seawater from the after compartments up the bow section in the hopes the sub would level off. But even after a third of the seawater was moved higher, still no budging from the bottom.*

Then the alerted surface fleet finally found the emergency signal buoy and started contact with the flooded sub. They determined that they would attempt a rescue using tugs to pull the submarine from the bottom by passing a line under her fore-section, then use compressed air to blow the ballast tanks. Fortunately for them, the area would allow divers to assist, which they attempted to accomplish quickly. But in one instance a line snapped and broke a diver's leg, and the deep water made other divers experience decompression sickness. The stormy seas also weren't helping matters, but after many problems with air hoses and even the radio line parting, a steel cable was attached to the sub and she was pulled up slowly using tugs. By a miracle, the ballast tanks were successfully blown and the sub came to surface. The entire operation took over three days to accomplish, but with extra air and food they all managed to survive, and even held a celebration by roasting a pig ashore after being towed safely back to base.

Early Soviet Spying:

Both of our countries during the Cold War were engaged in various spy activities against each other, and for good reasons. It was much easier to eavesdrop for secret information or to pay a foreign spy for technical details than to develop them ourselves. One of our early covert successes actually started in late 1945, when as a gift of friendship, our country gave the US Ambassador Averell Harriman a special plaque that represented our successful collaboration at winning World War Two. He proudly accepted the plaque and placed it on the wall inside the study at his residence in Moscow, a location where many diplomats met with him to discuss foreign policy and secret matters concerning us. What the American Ambassador didn't know though was the plaque was actually a passive *listening device which allowed us to hear many of his private conversations up until 1952, when it was finally discovered to be a listening device.*

Another example occurred in 1958 when one of our KGB agents in America approached a sergeant named Jack Dunlop who worked at the National Security Agency building in Fort Mead, MD as a messenger, and offered him a wealthy salary to pass along secret documents to us. He readily accepted this offer, and later began to copy documents that were being delivered between the various NSA departments, many of which were labeled Top Secret, and then gave these copies to our contacts, who then sent the information off to Moscow. Of important note was these documents were not encoded in any way, they were all written using plain English. This internal spy was so bold as to even take documents from department secretaries with promises to deliver them on his schedule, then use copy machines to make duplicates for us. This arrangement with him only lasted a couple of years before he was reassigned and eventually exposed, however obtaining these secret documents from the very building that produced them was one of our greatest spying achievements of the era.

First Phase Summary:

The Soviet responses to new military threats and changes brought about by the advent of atomic power started to cause doubts about the fundamental assumptions on which their naval construction program had earlier been based. Soviet leaders recognized that nuclear warfare had created an entirely new situation in which submarines could serve as strategic weapons, and small, missile-equipped surface ships could become the equal of much larger conventionally armed vessels. This resulted in four general phases with their submarine development. During this first phase, which took place from 1950 to 1957, over two-hundred and seventy diesel-powered submarines were built for interdicting sea lines of communication and for the defense of the sea approaches to the USSR. However, the Soviets realized that the US carrier fleet was becoming a dangerous threat to their mainland, so this led to their next phase, which was to develop anti-carrier capabilities.

1958-1966 Phase
The Development of Anti-Carrier Capabilities:

In order to meet the growing carrier threat posed by the United States, the Soviet Union created new classes of submarines meant to strike US carriers prior to any aircraft being launched. US naval forces at sea were often under Soviet surveillance and would be closely monitored during any periods of tension, eliminating the need for any pre-strike reconnaissance. Any US forces within launch range of Soviet territory at the outbreak of hostilities would be attacked almost immediately by these anti-carrier attack submarines. This anti-carrier capability was created from 1958 to 1966 during this second phase of submarine evolution, which included Soviet cruise missile and ballistic missile units, along with new torpedo attack units. Two of these, the Foxtrot and Romeo classes, were diesel-powered, while the November class was the first Soviet nuclear-powered submarine to be entered into service.

1958 Foxtrot Class

The Foxtrot class SS (*Project 641*) was designed as a replacement over the earlier Zulu class torpedo attack submarines which had suffered from structural weaknesses, including vibration problems. The first Foxtrot unit became operational in 1958. (See Figure 5 on page 13.) Their submerged speed was only 15 knots, while they had a length of 294 feet. Their operating depth limit was 920 feet. Just like the Zulu submarines, these were also diesel electric and had six 21-inch torpedo tubes at the bow, with four at the stern. They could carry up to twenty-two torpedoes. The Foxtrot class was considered a large submarine for carrying out longer patrols away from the Soviet coastline as an anti-ship submarine. Later Foxtrot units received upgraded diesel engines and further modernization, but by the time the last units were released, they were already considered obsolete due to easy enemy detection. Seventy-five Foxtrot submarines eventually entered service, and each carried a crew of seventy-two.

1958 Romeo Class

Another of the replacement torpedo attack submarines produced by the Soviet Union was the Romeo class SS (*Project 633*). The diesel-powered Romeo class was based on the earlier Whiskey class design. (See Figure 9.) They started entering service in 1958 and had a submerged speed of 13 knots. They included an overall length of 252 feet which was considered a medium-sized submarine of the newer post-World War Two designs, and were the first to have an air-foam fire extinguishing system. For armament they had six 21-inch torpedo tubes at the bow and two at the stern, with room to carry up to fourteen torpedoes. They had an operating depth limit of 980 feet. Twenty units entered service from 1958 to 1962, and each carried a crew of fifty-two. The Romeo class was discontinued from a planned fifty-six units due to performance issues with their diesel engines, the weaker batteries, and outdated torpedoes. But the main reason was the potential the Soviet Union saw with the arrival of nuclear submarines, such as the November class, which was released at the same time.

Figure 9. The Romeo class diesel-powered submarine was an improved version of the Whiskey class--it could dive deeper and remain submerged longer.

Figure 10. The November class was the first Soviet nuclear-powered submarine, and required many improvements during their early years of operation.

1958 November Class

The November class SSN (*Project 627 Kit*) was the first Soviet nuclear-powered torpedo attack submarine to enter into service. (See Figure 10.) The first November class unit became operational in 1958 with an impressive submerged speed of 30 knots, which was capable of keeping pace with US carriers. They had an overall length of 352 feet, and an operating depth limit of 1000 feet. Each unit had eight 21-inch torpedo tubes at the bow, and room to carry up to twenty torpedoes. This was the first Soviet sub to be able to launch torpedoes at depths down to 320 feet. The first unit K-3 was plagued with safety issues and was later named the *Leninsky Komsomol*. A typical problem experienced during early patrols with K-3 was the unreliability of her steam generators within the nuclear propulsion plant. This issue was later resolved with certain modifications, and translated into all later November class versions being designated *Project 627A*. Fourteen November class submarines entered service from 1958 to 1966, and each carried a crew of eighty-six.

The Soviet November class attempted to live up to its potential for endurance and distance through trial and error, but remained a first generation nuclear submarine requiring many improvements during their early years in operation. However, this was countered by occasional feats of endurance using this class to travel such areas as the North Pole or around South America. Four November units were eventually based in the Pacific Fleet—with three of those operating under Arctic ice—but most were based in the Northern Fleet. Both the November and Foxtrot classes were considered improvements for Soviet interdiction capabilities, while the Romeo class was an improvement over the Whiskey class, since they could operate at increased depths for greater periods of time.

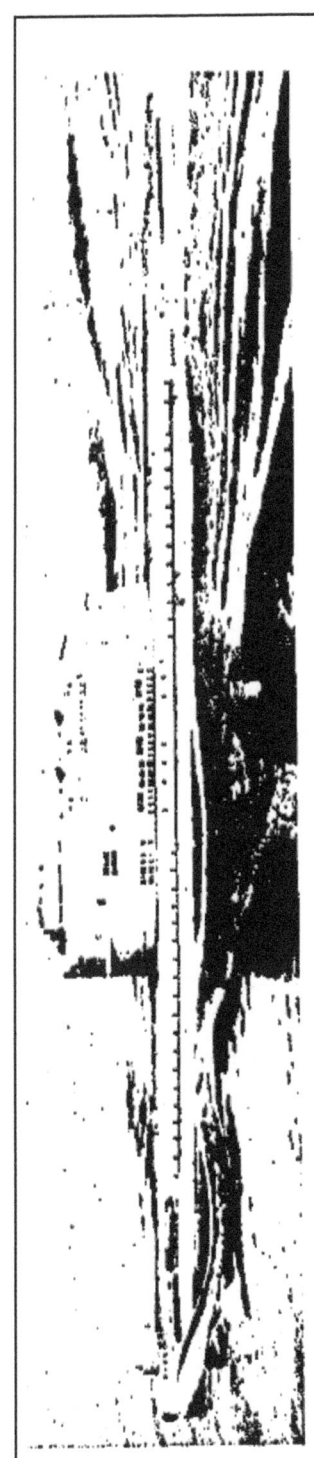

Figure 11. The Golf class was the first Soviet diesel-powered ballistic missile submarine. It carried three ballistic missiles that were housed in silos, but were launched while surfaced.

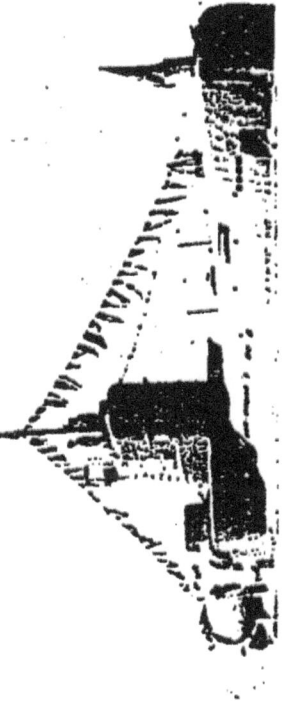

Figure 12. Some Whiskey class submarines were converted to fire cruise missiles from a surfaced position. The Twin Cylinder conversion, shown above, had two missile tubes on deck behind the sail.

Another new submarine, the Golf-I class, was the next to enter service as the first diesel-powered ballistic missile submarine.

1958 Golf-I Class

The Golf-I class SSB (*Project 629*) was a diesel-powered submarine built to carry three SS-1b Scud ballistic missiles. The basic design of this submarine got inspiration from the Foxtrot class, with the addition of three vertical silos just behind the sail. (See Figure 11.) The submerged speed of the Golf-I class was 12 knots, while they had a length of 323 feet. Their operating depth limit was 985 feet. The first three units of the Golf-I class were built to carry the SS-1b Scud ballistic missile, and twenty units were later built to carry the improved SS-N-4 ballistic missile. In order to launch a ballistic missile, the Golf-I submarine had to surfaced and have the missile raised above the sail. All versions had four 21-inch torpedo tubes at the bow, with two at the stern. They could carry up to six torpedoes. Twenty-three Golf-I class submarines entered service from 1958 to 1962, and each unit carried a crew of eighty. The Golf-I showed that the Soviet Union was able to create their first dedicated ballistic missile submarine, and a year later in 1959 the Soviet efforts to launch cruise missiles from submarines also became successful with the arrival of the SS-N-3 cruise missile.

SS-N-3 Cruise Missile:

The SS-N-3 Shaddock was the first long-range surface-launched cruise missile to enter service in the Soviet submarine fleet. Its unique design had wings which deployed after launch, and each had a maximum range of 250 nm at speeds up to Mach 0.9.

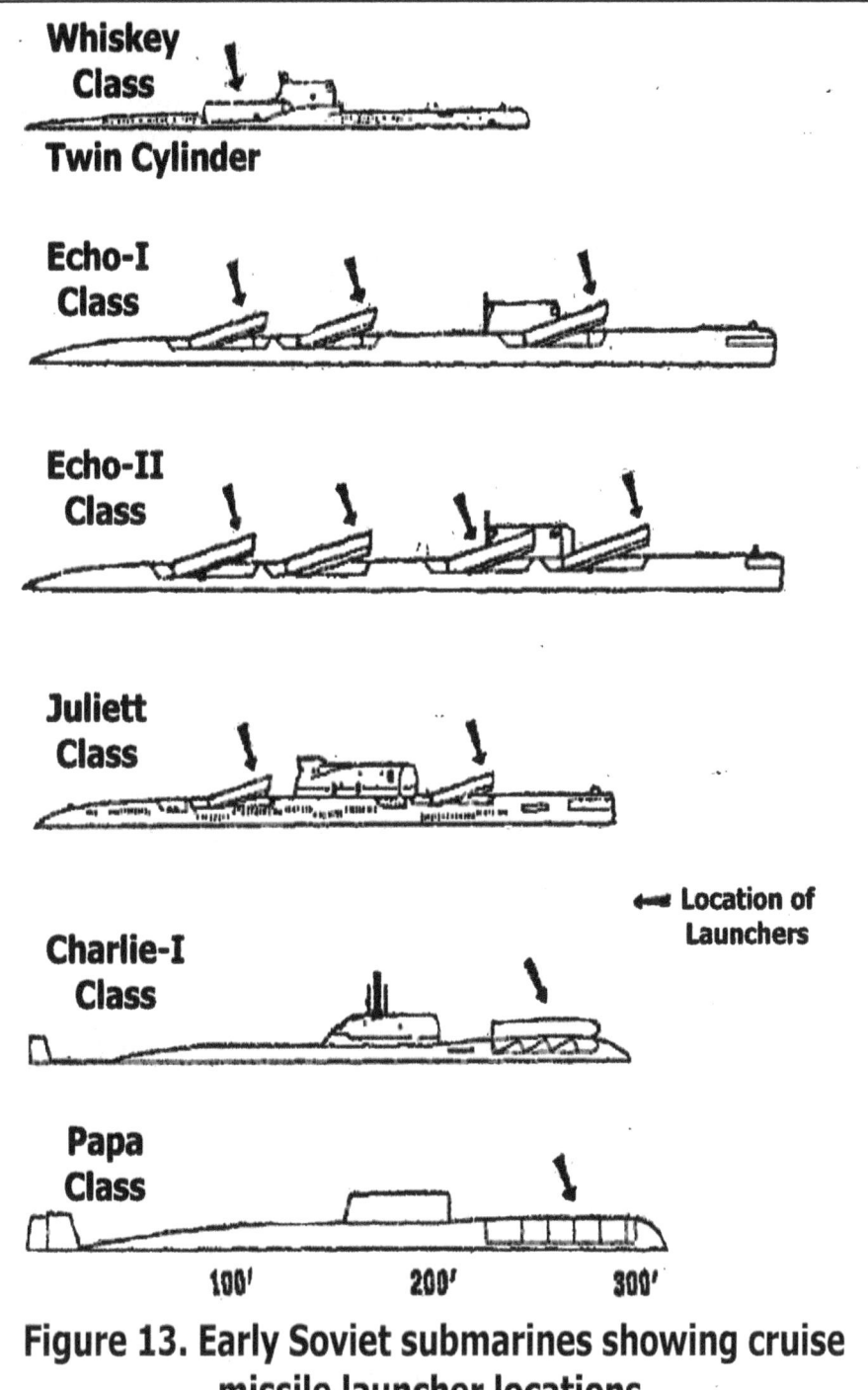

Figure 13. Early Soviet submarines showing cruise missile launcher locations.

Versions of this missile were fired from either ships or submarines, and it was developed into three major variants. The SS-N-3c Shaddock (*P-5*), the SS-N-3a Shaddock (*P-6*), and the SS-N-3b Nepal (*P-35*). The SS-N-3 had a similar turbojet engine as the MIG-19 fighter aircraft. When launched, the missile followed a flight path determined by its preset autopilot. The SS-N-3 had a homing radar for terminal guidance, and required a mid-course update. One land variant of the SS-N-3 was designed for use in coastal defense.

The Shaddock was designed to hit targets at a long range beyond the horizon of the launcher. The SS-N-3 system was limited by an inability to fire effectively at closer ranges. The missile's trajectory and its guidance system design were such that the missile had to travel at least 10 nm before its homing radar could acquire a target. The SS-N-3 missile in midcourse flight was not a difficult target for enemy air defenses. It flew at an altitude and speed comparable to that of the early jet fighters, and it lacked any evasive maneuverability. Submarines carrying these cruise missiles required approximately thirty minutes on the surface while preparing to fire, which was a major weakness. This resulted in further development towards a submerged firing version of cruise missiles. The first Soviet cruise missile system was a combination of the SS-N-3 and the Whiskey class submarines. Existing Whiskey submarines were modified to carry one, two, or four launch tubes. In some cases, the launch tubes were added to the deck, and in other cases they were built into an extended sail.

1959 Whiskey Single Cylinder

The Whiskey Single Cylinder submarine (*Project 613*) SSG was a regular Whiskey class submarine which was modified to carry a single SS-N-3c Shaddock cruise missile. A launch tube for the missile was placed just aft of the sail. Just one conversion of this type was ever completed in 1959.

1960 Whiskey Twin Cylinder

Another of the cruise missile conversions produced by the Soviet Union a year later was the Whiskey Twin Cylinder submarine (*Project 644*) SSG. This was a regular Whiskey Class submarine with two missile tubes added behind the sail. Only six units of this type were converted from 1960 to 1962. (See Figure 12.)

1961 Whiskey Long Bin

The Whiskey Long Bin submarine (*Project 665*) SSG was the final of the three Whiskey class conversions to carry the SS-N-3c Shaddock cruise missiles. This variant received an extended sail that carried four missiles, but the additional modifications caused stability problems. (See Figure 14.) Only six units of this type were converted from 1961 to 1963.

Since all the Soviet Whiskey class conversion submarines had to surface before they could launch an SS-N-3 cruise missile, they became vulnerable to detection and attack by enemy forces. The Soviets attempted to counter this vulnerability by keeping surface-to-air missile ships in or near the submarine launch areas. The Soviets generally used the same strike tactics for the surface-launched SS-N-3 missile system. Although targeting information for firing the SS-N-3 could be supplied by any appropriately positioned aircraft, surface ship, or submarine, the preferred tactic involved the use of a Bear D aircraft, which was a reconnaissance variant of the TU-95 heavy bomber. It could provide targeting data for any Whiskey SSG submarine located about 150 nm from the target. When possible, firings from two or more Whiskey SSG submarines required coordination so that their cruise missiles arrived on target nearly simultaneously and from different directions.

The SS-N-3 cruise missile could be launched while under favorable sea conditions at ranges up to 250 nm. The vulnerability to any launching Whiskey submarine would generally decrease with an increase in the target's range, however this further complicated the target acquisition problem, with the coordination of strikes using widely separated forces also becoming more difficult. In addition, as the missile flight times increased the defending forces would have a better chance at missile interception, while attacks from shorter ranges would be more vulnerable to counterattack, because the submarine needed enough time to surface, launch, and then provide initial guidance to the SS-N-3 missile.

A surfaced Soviet submarine could be defended by a surface combatant armed with surface-to-air missiles, and SAM-armed ships were often operated in conjunction with cruise missile submarines. This tactic was not always practicable, however, and the presence of the surface ship would be counter-productive if it attracted the attention of defending enemy forces. In the meantime, several new classes of cruise missile submarines were being developed while the conversions of the Whiskey class submarines were underway.

As the Soviet Navy was acquiring increasingly effective weapons like the SS-N-3 cruise missile, successful ballistic missile flight testing of the SS-N-4 Sark (*R-13*) continued, along with designing of the SS-N-5 Serb (*R-21*) missile. Flight-testing of the SS-N-4 was commenced at Kapustin Yar in June of 1959, and in the Northern Fleet later that same year. An operational capability with the weapon was achieved later in 1960. Further development also continued on the 650-nm-range SS-N-5 Serb ballistic missile. Detailed design and fabrication had started in 1959.

Figure 14. Long Bin was another Whiskey class conversion to fire cruise missiles while surfaced. It had four missile tubes built into an oversized sail.

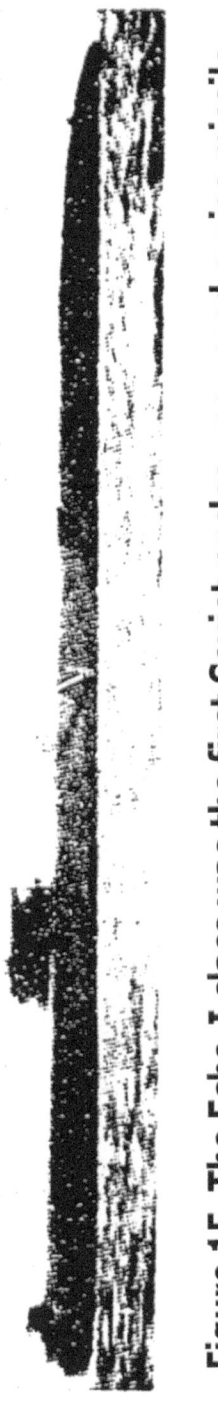

Figure 15. The Echo-I class was the first Soviet nuclear-powered cruise missile submarine. The submarine had to surface to fire its missiles.

Meanwhile, the first submarine specifically constructed to carry cruise missiles was the nuclear-powered Echo-I, with six missile tubes being built into the superstructure of the submarine. This program was followed by the nuclear-powered Echo-II using eight missile tubes, and the diesel-powered Juliett submarine with four missile tubes. All of these submarines carried variants of the SS-N-3 cruise missile which would replace the Whisky conversion program. (See Figure 13 for early submarines that carry cruise missiles.)

1960 Echo-I Class

The Echo-I class SSGN (*Project 659*) was a nuclear-powered submarine built to carry six SS-N-3c Shaddock cruise missiles housed in launchers. These needed to be tilted up fifteen degrees before firing. (See Figure 15.) These missiles could only be fired in a certain sequence, and required a few minutes of preparation time prior to launching, with the bearing for the launch being the same as the heading of the submarine. The Echo-I class had a submerged speed of 25 knots, while they had a length of 365 feet. In addition to the cruise missiles, they each had four 21-inch and two 15.7-inch torpedo tubes at the bow, with two more at the stern. Each could carry up to sixteen torpedoes, while their operating depth limit was 985 feet. Only five units of the Echo-I class were ever built, and all five were deployed in the Pacific Fleet for potential cruise missile strikes against the US west coast. However, due to the general ineffectiveness of the SS-N-3c cruise missile against certain targets, two more submarine classes—being the Echo-II and Juliett—emerged two years later.

1962 Echo-II Class

Figure 16. The Echo-II class nuclear-powered cruise missile submarine was similar to the Echo-I but had eight missile tubes.

Figure 17. The Juliett class was a diesel-powered cruise missile submarine that had four missile tubes for surface launching.

The Echo-II class SSGN (*Project 675*) was similar to the Echo-I, but carried eight of the improved SS-N-3a Shaddock cruise missiles that also tilted up to fire. (See Figure 16.) These anti-ship missiles were meant to be fired at US carriers in two volleys of four missiles each, after the necessary preparations were made once the submarine had surfaced. The only drawback with this update compared to the Echo-I was the slightly longer timeframe needed for preparing a launch. For additional armament they had four 21-inch torpedo tubes at the bow, and two 15.7-inch torpedo tubes at the stern, with room to carry up to ten torpedoes. They had a submerged speed of 23 knots, and an overall length of 378 feet, which was thirteen feet longer than the Echo-I due to the additional missile pair. Twenty-nine units entered service from 1962 to 1968, and each carried a crew of 104. Meanwhile, another submarine, the Juliett class, was also released the same year as the Echo-II, and was also meant for defense against US aircraft carriers.

1962 Juliett Class

The Juliett class SSG (*Project 651*) was a diesel-powered guided cruise missile submarine that was built for nuclear strikes against US aircraft carriers using four SS-N-3c Shaddock missiles. (See Figure 17.) The first Juliett class submarine entered service in 1962 based on similar designs of the Echo class, and had a submerged speed of 18 knots. They had an overall length of 295 feet, and an operating depth limit of 1000 feet. In addition to carrying cruise missiles, they each had six 21-inch torpedo tubes at the bow, and four 15.7-inch tubes at the stern. Each carried up to eighteen torpedoes, along with a crew of seventy-eight. Only sixteen units were built in the following six years before they were eventually phased out due to submerged-launched cruise missiles.

Figure 18. The Hotel class was the first Soviet nuclear-powered ballistic missile submarine and was based on the November design. Three versions were produced.

Figure 19. The nuclear-powered Hotel-II class submarine carried three SS-N-5 ballistic missiles which could be launched while submerged. These were modified versions of the Hotel-I class.

However, the Soviet Union still saw the importance of developing further diesel submarines while they had nuclear-powered units being constructed. Diesel submarines like the Juliett class were cheaper to produce, and cheaper to operate—being about one-third the cost of nuclear-powered submarines—but economics apparently weren't the main reason. The Soviets still needed enough diesel submarines to operate in case any major setbacks occurred within their nuclear program. The first nuclear-powered submarines they already used—the November class—still had their difficulties, especially with sporadic breakdowns in the propulsion system. And their early operations remained somewhat cautious, with November class submarines being closely followed by surface ships for assistance when needed.

While the Soviets had suddenly improved their anti-carrier capabilities through the use of nuclear propulsion and cruise missile classes, these achievements were quickly overtaken by a naval threat more potent than the aircraft carrier—it was the US Polaris ballistic missile submarines. These US submarines not only had more strategic strike potential than an aircraft carrier, but were more difficult to detect and track. The Soviet attack submarines developed for interdiction and anti-carrier missions had only limited anti-submarine warfare (ASW) capabilities, and had little ability to cope with the US Polaris ballistic missile force when they entered service in 1960. However, the Soviet Union countered that potential when their first nuclear-powered ballistic missile submarines also entered service at the same time.

1960 Hotel-I Class

The Hotel-I class SSBN (*Project 658*) was the first nuclear-powered ballistic missile submarine to operate in the Soviet Navy. (See Figure 18.)

Designation	IOC	Diameter (inches)	Length (feet)	Propulsion	Range/Speed (Yards)/(Kts)	Guidance	Warhead Weight (pounds)
533 mm (21 inch) Anti-Ship Torpedo Evolution							
53-57	1957	21	25	Kerosene Hydrogen Peroxide Turbine	20,000/45	Unguided	672
53-61	1961	21	25	Kerosene Hydrogen Peroxide Turbine	16,400/55	Acoustic Wake Following	672
53-65	1965	21	23.6	Kerosene Hydrogen Peroxide Turbine	20,000/45	Acoustic Wake Following	661
53-65K	1969	21	23.6	Kerosene Oxygen Turbine	20,800/45	Acoustic Wake Following	661
650 mm (25.6 inch) Anti-Ship Torpedo Evolution							
65-73	1973	25.6	36	Kerosene Hydrogen Peroxide Turbine	54,700/50	Unguided	Nuclear
65-76	1976	25.6	36	Kerosene Hydrogen Peroxide Turbine	54,700/50	Acoustic Wake Following	992

Figure 20. The 21-inch and 25.6-inch evolution of anti-ship torpedoes advanced from unguided versions to those using acoustic wake following.

The first Hotel-I class submarine entered service in 1960 based on overall designs of the November class, but had the silo structure of the Golf class. Therefore, each unit carried three SS-N-4 Sark (*R-13*) ballistic missiles which could only be fired from the surface. These were the first units to have a nuclear power-plant twin design, and were meant as a ballistic missile substitute for the November class. The Hotel-I submarines had a submerged speed of 26 knots, with an overall length of 374 feet. In addition to the ballistic missiles, they each had four 21-inch torpedo tubes at the bow, and two additional 15.7-inch torpedo tubes at both the bow and the stern. Each carried up to sixteen torpedoes. They had a depth limit of 985 feet, and carried a crew of 104. Only eight Hotel-I units were built from 1960 to 1962. The Hotel-II class (*Project 658M*) closely followed from 1963 to 1967 with seven of the eight Hotel-I units being upgraded to carry three SS-N-5 (*R-21*) ballistic missiles, which could be launched while submerged. These submarines also carried the newer 53-61 anti-ship torpedoes which used wake following for homing. (See Figure 19.)

Advancements With Anti-Ship Torpedoes:

In 1961 the Soviet Union successfully produced their first anti-ship torpedo having a more reliable propulsion method, created from the earlier SAET variants. This 53-61 version was a 21-inch diameter torpedo that also had an improved type of homing system. Instead of being a passive acoustic design, it used acoustic wake following to track a ship to explode at its stern. This was accomplished by the 53-61 torpedo sending impulses out after launch until it homed in on the wake of the ship, then tracked it from side-to-side as it followed through the wake to the stern before exploding. The main drawback for the 53-61 torpedo was it had to be

...ied from a close enough distance to acquire the ship's ...e. This left the attacking submarine vulnerable to ...ounter-attack. (See Figure 20 on anti-ship torpedo evolution.) This wake following method became the main homing system used in Soviet anti-ship torpedoes up until the end of the Cold War.

Troubles With Soviet Nuclear Submarines:

The Soviet sailors worked under hazardous conditions aboard their earliest nuclear submarines, since the success of the US fleet often spurred the Soviet political planners to insist on using rapid design and construction methods. One Soviet source claimed that their first nuclear subs had serious deficiencies because of their dangerous boilers. Another source was even more critical when claiming they had atomic submarines, but submariners had nothing good to say about them.

Another report talked about the troubles with the nuclear reactors and their ventilation systems. One crew reportedly had to be hospitalized for radiation sickness, and an officer was said to have been killed in a reactor accident. In 1958 a nuclear submarine was unable to surface for a prolonged period, and many crewmembers were affected by the foul air inside the boat. Because of such incidents, all those working aboard Soviet nuclear submarines at this time received a special bonus known as childlessness pay, an amount which doubled their regular salary. They also earned three years of longevity for every year they served on a nuclear submarine.

These regulations were eventually abandoned, but the Soviets still customarily sent a rescue ship along with nuclear submarines for their assistance on long-range patrols.

Submarine Spending in the USSR Navy:

Although the Soviet Union didn't seem to have a fixed budget ceiling on their naval spending during this phase, estimates of the value of this procurement showed a relatively stable outlay of about $1.4 billion annually in US dollar equivalents. This expenditure pattern reflected stable proportions of about fifty percent being devoted to nuclear submarines, about twenty percent to conventional submarines, and the remaining thirty percent to surface ships. There were no significant changes in this pattern when construction programs were shifted among cruise-missile submarines or ballistic-missile submarines. It seemed that Soviet naval planners viewed this mixture of diesel and nuclear-powered submarines as being the best combination in order to achieve their broader naval mission. Meanwhile, classified writings by high ranking Soviet officials stated that they were concentrating the responsibilities of the Navy into a more potent US carrier interdiction force.

This may well have been one of a series of decisions, including the establishment of the Strategic Rocket Troops and other organizational changes within their armed forces, which were announced by Khrushchev in January of 1960. Meanwhile the implementation of more advanced ballistic missile units continued, and it was known that by mid-1963 the SS-N-4 had been deployed aboard five Zulu-V class submarines, and in twenty of the twenty-three Golf-I class submarines, along with all eight of the Hotel-I class submarines. Further development also continued on the follow-up 650-nm-range SS-N-5 Serb (*R-21*) ballistic missile. A detailed design and fabrication was completed in early 1962 after the successful launching of thirty-five test missiles from a modified Golf class submarine. The following year they were implemented into the Hotel-II class.

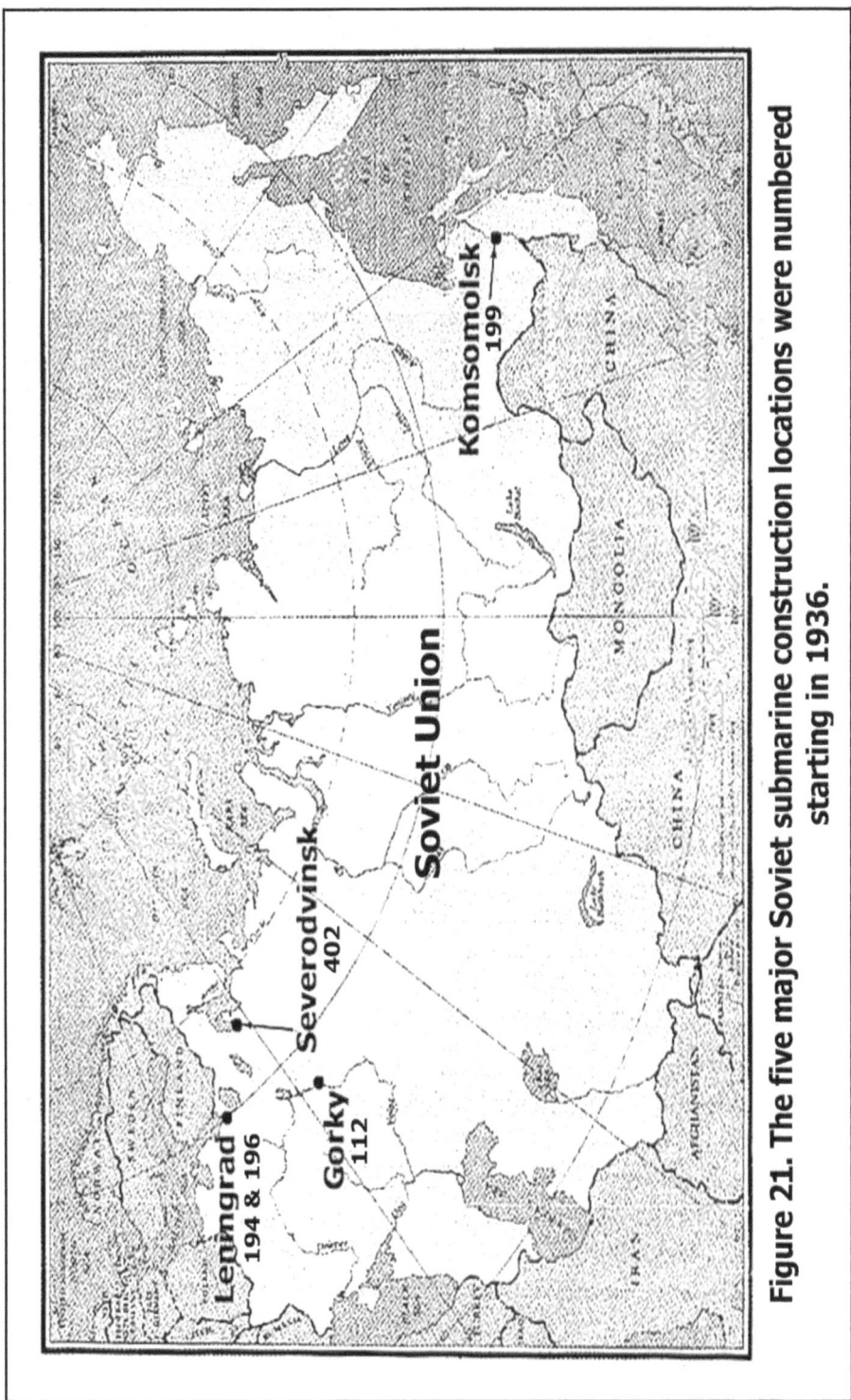

Figure 21. The five major Soviet submarine construction locations were numbered starting in 1936.

Soviet Submarine Construction Sites:

During the course of these phases, there were five major submarine shipyards that the Soviet Union used for building their various submarine classes. The first was the Gorky Shipyard–112, which was founded in 1849 on the west bank of the Volga River. Its location was on the northwest edge of the city of Gorky during the Soviet Union. It had first started as a machine factory, and later shifted to commercial shipbuilding, then converted over to military and submarines after World War Two. The second one was Komsomolsk Shipyard–Amur 199, which was founded inland on the north bank of the Amur River in 1932, and was the only submarine construction yard in the Soviet Far East. The third one was Leningrad Shipyard–Admiralty 194, which was founded by Peter the Great on the east bank of the Neva River in 1704, which was in the west-central part of the city of Leningrad during the Soviet Union. The fourth one was Leningrad Shipyard–Sudomekh 196, it was founded in the 1930's as a specialized submarine shipyard next to Admiralty 194 on the south bank of the Neva River. The fifth one was Severodvinsk Shipyard–402. It was founded nineteen miles west of Arkangelsk on the White Sea as a general military shipyard in 1939. The large scale production of submarines at this facility was started in the early 1950s.

Of the five shipyards engaged in the construction of Soviet submarines during 1961, three of them were producing cruise-missile submarines, one was producing torpedo-attack submarines, and one was producing both types. (See Figure 21 showing shipyard locations.) With the exception of the Juliett program at the Baltic Shipyard, it was expected that all of the cruise-missile submarine programs—the Echo-II class program at the Severodvinsk Shipyard and at Komsomolsk, and the Juliett class program in Gorky, would continue through 1968. The construction of the Echo-II class was originally authorized somewhat later than the Juliett program. Construction was started in the Baltic Shipyard in 1960, and in Shipyard 112 in Gorky in 1961. Neither of these two shipyards had produced submarines since the termination of the Whiskey class submarine program in 1957. The construction rate for these shipyards was two per year at the Baltic Shipyard, and about three to four per year at Gorky. The earlier program for the conversion of the Whiskey class submarines to Twin Cylinder and Long Bin types to carry cruise missiles had already ended by this time.

A Nuclear Reactor Accident:

*O*ur *Soviet government kept a secret from the general population for nearly thirty years about the reactor accident that occurred on July 4th, 1961, aboard our Hotel class nuclear submarine K-19. This happened while she was out participating in exercises in the North Atlantic, after having already completed drills that were scheduled earlier. As she was moving again to practice missile launches from beneath the Arctic sea, suddenly in the early morning the port reactor sounded an alarm. This was one of the first nuclear submarines constructed for our Soviet Navy, and experiences with malfunctions were not well tested. So when all the pumps that supported the coolant circulation stopped working, there was no recommendation on how to fix such a scenario. The situation was rapidly becoming life threatening for all aboard, and a solution to cool the port reactor was quickly required. It was determined that a secondary cooling system needed to be rapidly improvised using the onboard fresh water storage, but at a dangerous cost. All those that worked on such a system would likely receive fatal doses of radiation!*

Then a second problem became equally evident. They were stationed almost a thousand nautical miles away from the nearest Soviet base, and ice had somehow damaged the antennae to where they couldn't communicate with command ashore. The only option was to head to the exercise area and try to rendezvous with a Soviet surface ship, all the while attempting the repairs to implement a secondary cooling system. The grave detail of it cannot be overemphasized, but eight men placed themselves directly into the core to try and save their submarine, while other assisting crewmembers also received crippling doses of radiation. Fire broke out twice in the reactor room but was contained both times, and as men became seriously ill, others helped out. Then the emergency message was sent: Reactor accident. Crewmen sick. Need help. Latitude 66 North. Longitude 4 degrees. Commander. K-19. By a miracle contact was made with some nearby Soviet diesel submarines, and two of them quickly came to the rescue call. Upon their arrival an exchange of flares was made, while the stormy seas made transferring any sickened personnel from the nuclear sub extremely dangerous, but it was eventually accomplished.

But what to do next? It was impossible to tow the nuclear submarine due to the stormy conditions as they found out with each attempt. All that was left was to stabilize the nuclear sub, and then abandon her while the crew went aboard the waiting diesel sub. Two torpedoes were prepared in case the nearby American warships which were monitoring the situation devised a plan to attempt a "salvage." Luckily this was never required. Instead, a Soviet fleet rescue ship was dispatched and towed the stricken sub back to base, where she was eventually repaired and returned into service. Of the seamen originally aboard, the eight who went into the reactor core all rapidly died, and were buried shortly after returning to base. But their sacrifice wasn't in vain. Their plan was used in other nuclear submarines where a secondary cooling system was added for safety, so in some ways the story ends with lost lives helping to protect untold others. But none of the dead were rewarded as Heroes Of The Soviet Union by our government, the highest honor possible to be bestowed on any individual. Moscow instead didn't want to broadcast such a design failure to the rest of the world, and as such they were only decorated with medals for their bravery and sacrifice. Afterwards, when K-19 made her way back to sea, she was given the nickname "Hiroshima" by the veteran Soviet submariners, as a reference to the city bombed by America during the Second World War.

Dangers At The Dock:

While it seems normal to only consider the dangers that a submariner might encounter while being out at sea, sometimes something as simple as loading a torpedo at the dock might turn into a major catastrophe. One such accident happened in 1962 aboard our Soviet sub B-37 after the ensign was raised, and the order was given to begin jacking over equipment with weapons on power. Suddenly, there was a fire that broke out inside the sub in the torpedo compartment due to careless damage, and this resulted in a massive explosion that not only took out the forward section of the submarine, but also damaged another nearby submarine, including demolishing the nearby pier. In all over one-hundred personnel died that day, requiring all of the scattered remains to be hastily buried in a local cemetery. It was a reminder of how everyone must rely on others to be safe when loading weapons aboard, since any slight carelessness might end up killing an entire crew.

Early 1963 to 1965:

It was in early 1963 when the Soviet Navy began to broaden the strike mission role used by their missile submarine forces, and this revision was linked to a number of changes in national Soviet policies. After the Cuban Missile Crisis had ended in October of 1962, an intense debate was waged amongst the Soviet leadership until about May of 1963. This debate was concerned with the organization and control of national economic planning, the general allocation of these resources, and also a review of specific military objectives. An indication that the Navy's responsibilities were expanded during this time was given by the Soviet Navy's Commander-in-Chief Admiral Sergey Gorshkov. Earlier statements by this admiral generally were careful and restrained, but after the Cuban Missile Crisis they took on a stronger tone. Due to the success of their new nuclear program, he enabled the Soviet submarine force to do what was earlier considered impractical. He further emphasized this role of nuclear submarines for executing this mission against their most important land objectives deep within enemy territory. It was therefore noticeable when, in 1964 and 1965, their Soviet submarine out-of-area operations were increased considerably over earlier levels. The Navy's new aggressiveness was in part a consequence of the growth of technical and operational capabilities built up over many years, but was also a reflection of policy decisions made due to the outcome of the Cuban Missile Crisis itself.

Whereas there was little evidence before 1964 that the Soviet Navy could maintain an operational force some distance from local naval theaters for any length of time, a small force of diesel-powered submarines and surface ships in mid-1964 began transitioning to almost continuous operations in the Mediterranean by using supporting ships. In addition, out-of-area operations were a particularly critical factor with respect to their nuclear-powered submarines. Not until early 1965 was there any known out-of-area operations of nuclear-powered submarines, in which a submarine was not accompanied by a naval auxiliary unit for escort or support. More importantly, however, were the periodic patrols of five to six weeks duration being established by both ballistic-missile and cruise-missile submarines as far as a few hundred miles south of the Aleutians in the North Pacific, and as far south as the Azores in the central Atlantic. This strategy was reinforced after Premier Khrushchev fell from power on October 14th, 1964, and was replaced by Leonid Brezhnev.

1963 JFK Assassination:

It can't be passed by that during the Cold War the U.S. President John F. Kennedy was assassinated on November 22nd, 1963, while in Dallas, Texas, as he rode in the back of a limousine. It was done by an individual named Lee Harvey Oswald, who had wanted to return to our country with his family. The Warren Commission was set up by the United States government to investigate the whole affair, and came to many conclusions, but never cleared up the matter sufficiently for the American public to trust how it happened, or even why. Something as simple as who fired the rifle was still left up to speculation, instead of outlining enough of the critical facts. Many people might still not agree that there were only three bullets fired at JFK from the same location, since the first shot hadn't been accounted for properly by the commission. Not until many years later, some sleuthing uncovered the details of how this first bullet was actually a ricochet. Upon firing his rifle, the first bullet struck the top arm of the traffic light just above JFK's head at the intersection below the window that Lee Harvey Oswald used. From there, it glanced down in front of the limousine while missing JFK, then hit the curb and ricocheted again to hit the edge of a concrete underpass down the street. Also of note was Lee Harvey Oswald had talked with a KGB agent inside our Soviet Embassy in Mexico City a few weeks prior to the assassination. Was the U.S. government afraid to tell more about this for fear of nuclear war? Would the American public demand retaliation if the assassination was blamed on a foreign government agency?

Another interesting fact was how Lee Harvey Oswald himself was shot a few days after he was arrested while in Dallas police custody. The gunman Jack Ruby was allowed to enter the police building multiple times, and while pretending to be a reporter, he shot Lee Harvey Oswald in front of the gathered newspaper and television crews. This all must have seemed very convenient to everyone, meanwhile Lee Harvey Oswald was called a lone gunman for the JFK assassination, and it was left at that. Even our own government attempted to distance us from this, and rightly so. We even managed to level rumors about some possible CIA involvement with right wing advocates. Still, after many decades later, few people still trust the outcome of the investigation or who was blamed as the lone culprit.

Figure 22. A grainy photograph of a surfacing Juliett class Soviet submarine typical of the quality which U.S. intelligence were supplied with in the early years of military assessments.

More Submarine Casualties:

A Soviet submarine was lost with all hands in the Barents Sea in 1961, and in 1962 two Northern Fleet submarines reportedly suffered heavy damage and crew casualties due to dangerous ice conditions. The bulk of a Foxtrot class submarine was salvaged at Rosta after a collision with a merchant ship in early 1964. Some Foxtrot and Zulu class submarines being used on the longest patrols into the Pacific, Atlantic, and the Mediterranean, were photographed returning to base while remaining on the surface. They were unable to dive underwater to avoid observation because of visible damage to the air induction systems in their sails, perhaps caused by mechanical issues or heavy seas. Numerous minor breakdowns and accidents also were noted. A Foxtrot class submarine operating in the vicinity of the Quarantine Line near Cuba during the 1962 Missile Crisis was unable to submerge, and was escorted back to her home port by a rescue tug. A Whiskey class submarine on patrol near Japan in early 1963 was unable to submerge and had to return to Soviet waters while remaining on the surface. In early 1963 a Foxtrot class submarine was en route from where she was built in the Baltic to the Northern Fleet, when she damaged her bow in a collision with a Finnish merchant ship, and was forced to return to Leningrad. In August of 1963 a submarine being towed into Nakhodka appeared to have a rebuilt stern, possibly the result of an earlier collision.

Poor Resolution Photography:

Although grainy photographs supplied to US intelligence in mid-1964 showed units of a new class of large ballistic missile submarine being completed, this evidence of such a program remained at the time unverified. The original photographs consisted of four different observations of submarines which, by virtue of their apparent length and other features, appeared to be units of a new class. But further analysis of these observations—all of which were conducted using poor-quality photography—led to the conclusion that they were not a new class. This re-examination showed the limitations of relying only on low-resolution photography at the time. (See Figure 22.)

1965 Nuclear Construction Update:

Production of Soviet nuclear-powered submarines was held rather steady at about six units per year from 1961 to 1965. Only two shipyards, Severodvinsk and Komsomolsk, were engaged in the construction of nuclear-powered submarines, and there were no indications that more shipyards were being added. The average annual rate of construction was four units from Severodvinsk, and two units from Komsomolsk. (See Figure 23 for construction numbers.)

YEAR	52	53	54	55	56	57	58	59	60	61	62	63	64
USSR Submarines	0	0	0	0	0	0	1	2	4	8	13	19	25
Number of shipyards in program	0	0	0	0	1	2	2	2	2	2	2	2	2

Figure 23. The cumulative number of Soviet nuclear-powered submarines constructed from 1952 to 1964, with how many shipyards were in the program.

In 1965 there were two versions of submarine-launched cruise missiles in service: (1) the SS-N-3a, which had a 250 nm range and a low flight profile designed for targeting aircraft carriers, and (2) the SS-N-3c, which also had a 250-

nm range. All earlier cruise missile submarines were designed for firing the SS-N-3c, but only the nuclear-powered Echo-II class and later Juliett submarines were constructed for firing the SS-N-3a. (See Figure 24 on cruise missiles.)

Salvage Gone Awry:

The following account of a salvage operation gone awry illustrates several of the problems for which the Soviet Navy was vulnerable during various emergency situations. In December of 1965, a Northern Fleet freshwater distillation ship had gone aground in the Kola inlet, and a submarine rescue ship was sent out to offer them assistance.

Upon arrival, it was discovered that the distillation ship had a broken keel with a flooded engine room. The ship's crew had erected a tent-like shelter on the upper outside deck, and lit a fire underneath it to keep them warm in the meantime. In addition, they had become intoxicated from consuming the ship's entire monthly ration of alcohol meant for maintaining the working equipment. After the salvage party boarded the disabled ship, officers began issuing orders that were countermanded by other officers, resulting in mass confusion. There were some instances where officers performed work while sailors merely watched them. Then after twenty hours of pumping the engine room, most of the water had been removed.

At this point, however, pandemonium set in again. Funnels weren't available for refueling the pumps, and a decision was made to carry gasoline from a storage tank in buckets. Then fuel was spilled onto the hot pumps causing a fire, which rendered several of them inoperable. Spilling fuel also made the decks slippery, and several sailors sustained injuries from slipping and falling. Lubricating oil from the pump engines was used up, but no one had bothered replacing it, causing the remaining pumps to burn out. New pumps were brought to the scene and connected to the existing hoses, which by then had become frozen. Sections of hoses were disconnected and the ice inside was broken up using hammers—causing them to spring leaks. During this time, officers continued to countermand other officer's orders.

Eventually they got all the water pumped out, and a line was attached from a tugboat to the disabled ship. After several attempts, the ship was pulled free, but apparently the damaged hull wasn't properly patched, and the ship began to take on more water. The pumps couldn't keep up, and the ship settled deeper into the water. Additional pumps were brought aboard, and, after more pumping, pontoons were lashed alongside. Two weeks after the start of the salvage operation, the distillation ship was finally towed to port. However, the ship with the two pontoons attached was too large to allow her to tie up alongside a pier, and so the makeshift contraption had to be beached. A month later, the ship was towed to a floating dry-dock where she was finally repaired.

Soviet Force Capabilities:

By 1965 the Soviet Navy possessed about 385 submarines, 19 cruisers with two of them having guided missiles, 24 guided-missile destroyers, 140 other destroyers and destroyer escorts, and 2,700 patrol, mine warfare, amphibious, and auxiliary vessels, including 140 guided-missile patrol boats. These numbers reflected the world's largest mine warfare force, including the most ships with surface-to-surface missiles. They also had the only missile armed patrol boats, and the only cruise-missile-equipped submarines capable of attacking at ranges up to 250 nm. After a late start, the number of Soviet nuclear submarines almost equaled that of the United States, partly due to delays in the US nuclear program.

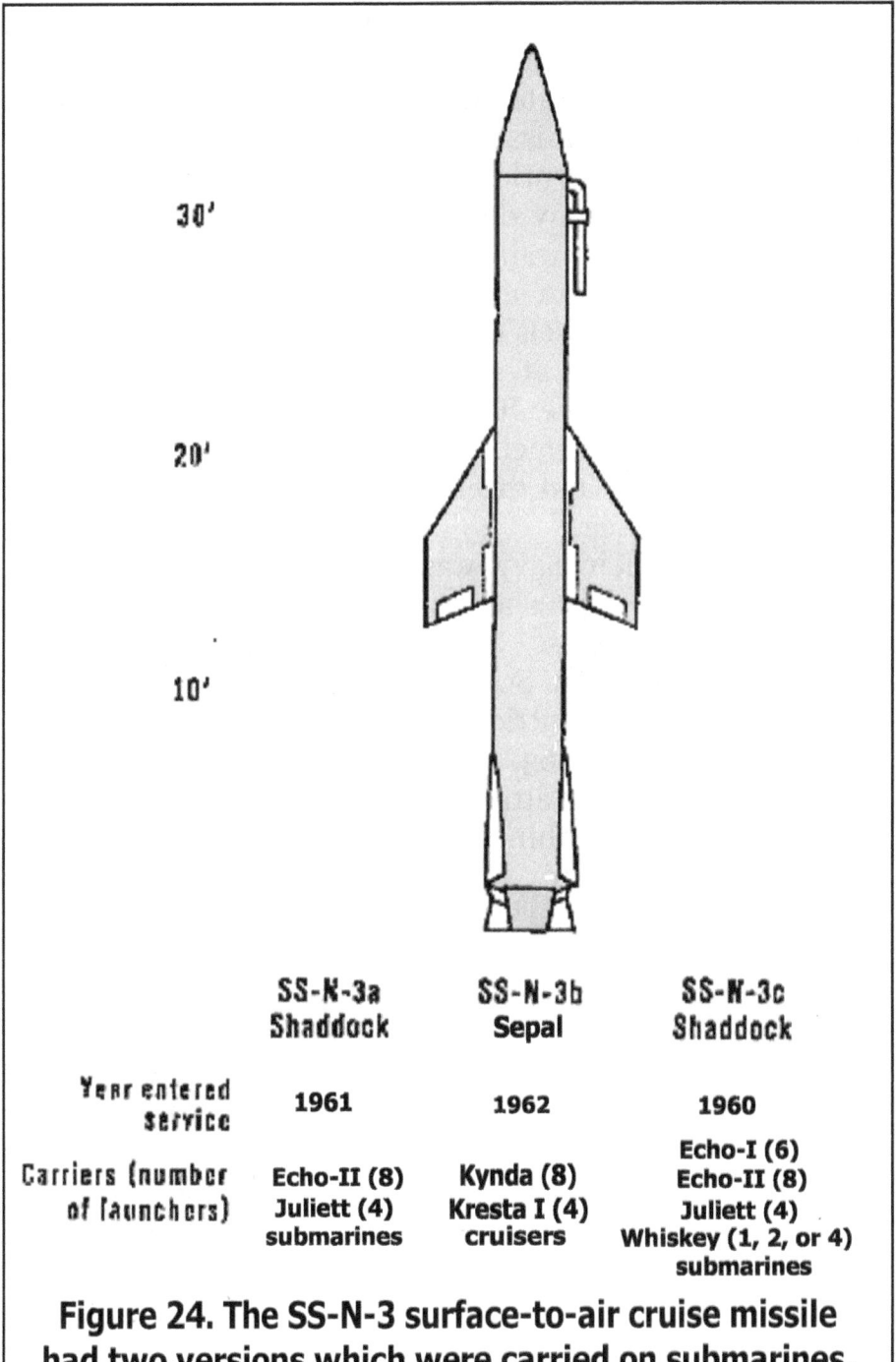

Figure 24. The SS-N-3 surface-to-air cruise missile had two versions which were carried on submarines, and one version which was carried on cruisers.

Having begun to construct such an impressive array of complex modern warships, the Soviets sought to increase their ability to operate those forces more effectively. Although the Soviets missed many of the lessons learned by other navies during World War Two, they made strenuous efforts to overcome any deficiencies. Operating areas were expanded, and joint training exercises were held. Soviet submarines also began extending their operations. Since 1963, Soviet naval vessels of all kinds started going to sea in greater numbers, and at greater distances from the USSR than ever before. Since June of 1964, Soviet surface ships and submarine detachments began operating frequently in the Mediterranean, and extensive exercises were conducted in the Norwegian Sea.

In addition, their navy was used for more diplomatic purposes, with Soviet naval vessels making formal port calls to countries such as Denmark, Norway, Yugoslavia, Rumania, and Bulgaria. Soviet naval research ships visited a number of African countries, in addition to Canada, the UK, and the US. After 1963, the number of days on distant patrols by the Soviet attack submarine force had already increased rapidly within a decade. The most dramatic increase was in the Mediterranean, where a small representation in the early 1960s had grown to be the most concentrated and continuous Soviet submarine patrol effort. Deployments into the Indian Ocean and into the Caribbean Sea followed later on.

The Soviet attack submarine force was gaining experience in conducting longer patrols with techniques of surveillance at sea, and frequently exercised anti-ship tactics and torpedo firings while using their available submarines–along with the increasing number of nuclear-powered units among them– for effective interdiction. As an example of this attack force potential, the Soviet Northern Fleet was able to maintain twenty-three long range submarines on continuous patrol in the North Atlantic, while the Pacific Fleet could maintain about thirteen long range attack submarines on continuous patrol as well.

Contending With US Carriers:

The Soviet cruise missile and torpedo attack submarine force was eventually sufficient in number and were fast enough to stalk the US carrier forces when at sea. These Soviet cruise missile submarines confronted the US carrier fleet with a complex defensive problem. While all the Soviet submarines still fired from the surface, the 250 nm range of the SS-N-3 missile afforded each attacker about 200,000 square nautical miles of possible positions from which to launch. Although this long range missile required targeting data assistance, such data could be obtained and transmitted by another submarine, or via an assisting aircraft. Observations of some cruise missile attack exercises indicated that the Soviets had developed tactics for coordinated surprise raids. These were carried out by their submarines using supporting aircraft or surface ships. The potential for a coordinated surprise raid was enhanced in the Mediterranean where US carriers were under constant surveillance, and their locations were usually known. Sonar conditions still favored the Soviet submarines there, and the continuous presence of the crowded naval forces would contribute to US uncertainties in recognizing the beginnings of an attack.

Soviet cruise missile attacks on US carriers in the Pacific and the Atlantic would be more difficult to achieve because US surveillance was generally more effective in those oceans than in the Mediterranean. The greater distances involved and the existence of US SOSUS arrays increased the probability of detecting a Soviet cruise missile submarine attempting to intercept a carrier group. The Soviet submarine might attempt to stalk the carrier before a coordinated strike for some time to assure itself of contact with the target at the moment a strike was ordered. If the Soviets deliberately initiated the hostilities, then coordinated missile attacks would be launched without warning. A trailing missile-armed ship might be the first to open fire. This attack would be accompanied by short-range missiles launched from submerged submarines, along with gunfire or short-range missiles from supporting surface ships. Longer-range missiles would then follow.

Even if the Soviets were not expecting hostilities, US carriers within or near launch range of Soviet territory would be most likely brought under attack. Such operations would not be as well coordinated as a preemptive attack, but would contain essentially the same elements. US carrier forces located at considerable distances at the outbreak of hostilities would pose a different problem. Although the Soviet forces would have more time to respond to them, such US forces would not be an immediate threat to Soviet territory. Soviet submarine exercises, and reactions to carrier task forces, showed that the greatest strike effort would be concentrated only against any US carriers within aircraft range of the Soviet Union. Afterwards, an echelon of Soviet cruise missile submarines would deploy into defensive barriers, presumably to interdict any US forces which had escaped an attack.

Anti-submarine Operations:

While Soviet anti-submarine operations were often hampered by inadequate surveillance in the early 1960s, a wide area ocean surveillance system such as SOSUS wasn't a practical system for the USSR to develop. Soviet technology wasn't capable of producing the sensitive hydrophones or cables needed to reach from potential SOSUS areas to the distant USSR mainland. Although overt and covert trailing offered them some promise, both methods were susceptible to countermeasures such as delousing.

533 mm (21 inch) Anti-Submarine Torpedo Evolution

Designation	IOC	Diameter (inches)	Length (feet)	Propulsion	Range/Speed (Yards)/(Kts)	Guidance	Maximum Launch Depth (Feet)	Warhead Weight (Pounds)
SET-53	1958	21	25.6	Electric Lead-Acid Battery	8,750/23	Passive Acoustic Homing	650	220
SET-53M	1964	21	25.6	Electric Silver-Zinc Battery	15,300/29	Passive Acoustic Homing	650	220
SET-65	1965	21	25.6	Electric Silver-Zinc Battery	17,500/40	Active/Passive Acoustic Homing	1,300	452
TEST-68	1969	21	25.9	Electric Silver-Zinc Battery	15,300/29	Passive Acoustic Wire Guided	650	220
TEST-71	1971	21	25.9	Electric Silver-Zinc Battery	16,400/40	Passive Acoustic Wire Guided	1,300	452
USET-80	1980	21	25.9	Electric Copper-Magnesium Battery	22,000/43	Acoustic Passive Active/Wake Following	1,300	440 to 660

Figure 25. The 21-inch evolution of Soviet anti-submarine torpedoes advanced from passive acoustic homing to include active acoustic and wake following.

Soviet submarines at this point were also too noisy for the covert detection of quieter US submarines. Soviet submarines instead focused on conducting reconnaissance in Western submarine patrol areas and transit routes. As the confidence and the ability of these patrols improved, Soviet attack submarines attempted more involved operations, including the trailing of Western submarines.

Other plans involved the development of titanium for use in pressure hulls for their submarines. The Soviet Union had a large titanium industry, and was already using this metal extensively within their shipbuilding industry. The lightness and strength of titanium created an increased depth capability, and resulted in extended sonar ranges and evasion potential. The Soviets also attempted to improve submarine command and control systems, and onboard tactical and machinery systems, through the use of onboard computers. Another prime area of interest was for progress with noise quieting. Soviet planners recognized quieting as a vital element for achieving suitable submarine ASW capabilities. Further submarine construction began showing noise quieting improvements over earlier submarine classes. In torpedo designs, the Soviet Union introduced a new model in 1965 which was electrically operated for use against enemy submarines. The SET-65 version contained batteries for power and ran quieter. It also only used electric motors for propulsion, along with active homing built into the nose of the torpedo for depth corrections. This was to become the standard ASW torpedo for use within the Soviet fleet. (See Figure 25 on the evolution of ASW torpedoes.)

Soviet Rescue and Salvage ships:

The Soviets in 1965 had some sixty rescue and salvage tugs, submarine rescue ships, and other auxiliaries of this type for use in rescue work.

Rescue Diving Platform

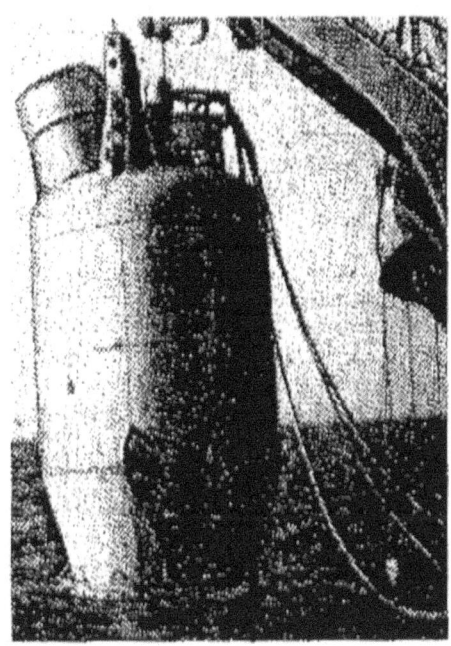
Soviet Rescue Chamber or Bell

Prut-Class Submarine Rescue Ship

Figure 26. Various Soviet rescue equipment used for recovery operations.

Soviet Escape Suit

Escape Training Tower

Soviet Recompression Chamber used to bring divers up from the depths

Figure 27. Various Soviet breathing equipment used for rescue, with an escape tower being used for training.

Most of this fleet was either built or converted since 1960, when the Soviets began modifying deck hatches on older submarines for bell or chamber rescue operations. The best vessel for use in Soviet rescue work was the 2,120-ton Prut class rescue ship. They were equipped with two diving chambers, two rescue chambers, an observation chamber, heavy mooring buoys, and air compressors. Several 840-ton T-58 minesweepers were also converted into rescue ships. These were equipped with a rescue bell and a diving bell. (See Figure 26 showing rescue equipment.)

Use of rescue equipment was often a regular part of the training program for all Soviet submariners. Escape towers used for practice had high structures resembling water towers. These were built for training at submarine schools and on the hull of a training submarine at Leningrad, and another one at Sevastopol. These allowed submariners to learn how to escape by flooding one compartment, then opening a hatch and swimming to the surface.

Their escape breathing apparatus consisted of a close-fitting rubber hood, an oxygen cylinder, and a canister for absorbing carbon dioxide. Similar equipment was used earlier by the US and UK navies, but was eventually replaced by buoyant free breathing hoods containing an initial charge of compressed air. (See Figure 27 on escape towers and breathing apparatus.)

Despite this individual Soviet training, however, the USSR never fully subscribed to the British theory that trapped submariners could best be saved through their own efforts. Rather, like the US, they tried when possible to rescue groups of personnel by using diving bells. Another advantage was their salvage tugs and other support vessels were constantly at sea in areas where Soviet submarines were patrolling, with rescue operations being possible down to depths of two-hundred meters (656 feet) using escape hatches and rescue buoys. (See Figure 28.)

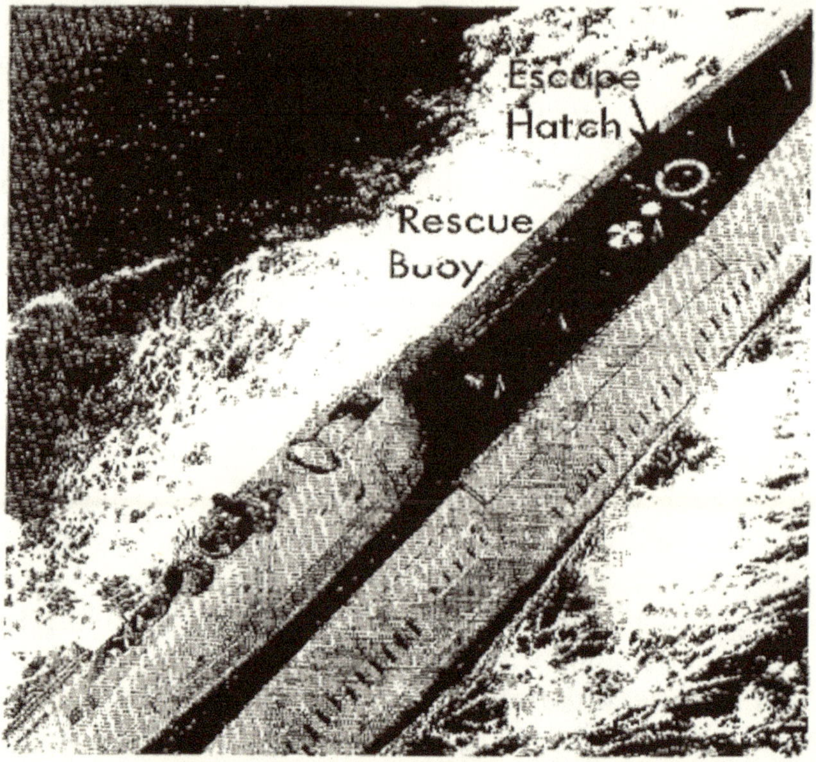

Juliett Class Cruise Missile Submarine

Romeo Class Torpedo Attack Submarine

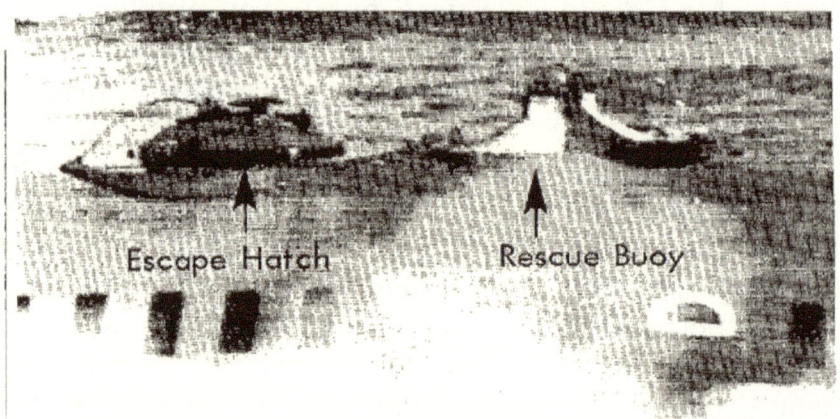

Figure 28. Escape equipment used on Soviet submarines including rescue buoy and escape hatch locations.

Second Phase Summary:

During the 1960s, the Soviet attack submarine force abandoned its pattern of local fleet area exercises for an ambitious program of distant area deployments. The evolution of the Soviet attack submarine force reflected changing naval threats. Soviet responses to new threats resulted in four general phases of submarine development. The first phase took place during 1950 to 1957, when nearly two-hundred and seventy diesel-powered submarines were built for interdicting sea lines of communication, and for the defense of the sea approaches to the USSR. During this second phase from 1958 to 1966, nuclear propulsion and cruise missiles were incorporated into Soviet submarines to meet the threat of US aircraft carriers. Some 130 submarines were built during this phase, with about fifty-five of those being cruise missile types. However, these Soviet achievements in nuclear propulsion and cruise missiles were overtaken by the need for a counter weapon to the US Polaris ballistic missile submarine force. This led to the next phase of the Soviet submarine fleet, the development of anti-submarine capabilities.

1967-1975 Phase Development of Anti-Submarine Capabilities:

During the third phase in Soviet attack submarine development, ASW improvements were enacted for enhancing underwater capabilities—which meant using advanced sonar, creating higher underwater speeds, increasing depth abilities and using newer weapons. This anti-submarine phase, which began in 1967 and lasted until 1975, created new classes of submarines to detect, intercept, and trail US submarines. In addition, in 1967 there was another Soviet submarine program ready to be launched—it was a Polaris-type submarine which carried sixteen ballistic missiles being built at the Severodvinsk shipyard by the White Sea, with the first unit of these—designated the Yankee class—being ready by the end of the year. A new Victor class submarine was also being built at the Admiralty shipyard in Leningrad.

1967 Victor-I Class

The Victor-I class SSN torpedo attack submarine (*Project 671 Yorsh*), the first unit of which was operational in 1967, represented the first Soviet attempt to develop an anti-submarine submarine. The Victor-I class was an improved version of the older November class units. (See Figure 29.)

Figure 29. The nuclear-powered Victor class submarine featured a teardrop shape which resulted in a faster Soviet submarine capable of speeds up to 32 knots.

Leningrad had a limited production capacity, and this building program was intended to produce only a limited number of submarines. The nuclear-powered Victor-I class was capable of 32 knots, and thus had the ability to trail US submarines overtly, however it was still noisier than comparable US attack submarines. There were sixteen units eventually produced, and each had a length of 305 feet. Their operating depth limit was 1310 feet. For armament each had six 21-inch torpedo tubes at the bow capable of launching anti-ship or ASW torpedoes such as the 53-65 or SET-65 versions. They could carry up to twenty-two torpedoes, and each carried a crew of sixty-eight. The Victor-I class frequently patrolled Western submarine transit routes. The Soviets made progress in quieting these submarines, but their noise levels were still higher than that of US nuclear submarines, and were considered too high for any covert trailing while remaining undetected.

1967 Yankee-I Class

The Yankee-I class SSBN (*Project 667A Navaga / Project 667AU Nalim*) was a 2nd generation of nuclear-powered submarines that carried surface launched ballistic missiles (SLBMs) comparable to the US Polaris submarines. (See Figure 30.) They were the first Soviet ballistic missile submarines to have sixteen SS-N-6 Serb (*R-27*) missiles fitted entirely within the hull. They also had four 21-inch torpedo tubes at the bow, and carried eighteen Type 53 anti-ship torpedoes, along with the SET-65 ASW torpedo. In addition, there were two other 15.7-inch torpedo tubes also at the bow. The Yankee-I class had a submerged speed of 28 knots, while they had a length of 433 feet. Their operating depth limit was 1312 feet, and each carried a crew of 114. Thirty-four Yankee-I class submarines were eventually built from 1967 to 1974, with twenty-two operating in the Northern Fleet, and twelve in the Pacific Fleet. Initially, the submarines were capable of firing four salvos of four ballistic missile each from an approximate ocean depth of 120 feet, but were later upgraded to launch two salvos of eight ballistic missiles each from the same depth. Many improvements were made in the construction program that eventually led to quieter Yankee class submarines. (See Figure 32 for ballistic missile submarine size comparison.) Another class of nuclear-powered attack submarine was released a year later–designated the Charlie-I class–and was being built at the Gorky shipyard.

1968 Charlie-I Class

The Charlie-I cruise missile class SSGN (*Project 670 Skat*) represented continuing efforts to meet the US carrier threat, but also had an ASW capability–primarily for self-protection. (See Figure 31.) The nuclear-powered Charlie-I, the first unit of which became operational in 1968, was an improved anti-ship and ASW submarine meant to replace the Echo class. The Charlie-I submarine carried eight SS-N-7 anti-ship cruise missiles which had a range of about 35 nm. They could be submerged launched, and required no external target acquisition platform. Earlier cruise missile submarines had to receive targeting information from another source, and also had to surface to fire their missiles.

The Charlie-I class had ASW capabilities either for self protection or for a secondary role as an ASW submarine. It was similar to the Victor-I class in such characteristics as hull streamlining, torpedo weapons system, and propulsion. The Charlie-I class, with a speed of 24 knots, was slower than the 32 knot Victor-I class. The Charlie-I started entering service in 1968, and they had an overall length of 312 feet. For armament each unit had six 21-inch torpedo tubes at the bow, with room to carry up to fourteen torpedoes. They had an operating depth limit of 985 feet. Eleven units entered service from 1968 to 1973, and each carried a crew of one-hundred.

The SS-N-7 Starbright (*P-70 Amethist*) cruise missile carried aboard the Charlie-I class was the first operational submarine cruise missile capable of being launched from underwater, and required no external guidance. At less than twenty-five feet long, it had solid booster and sustainer engines with supersonic flight speeds up to Mach 1.0.

Figure 30. The Yankee-I class nuclear-powered submarine carried sixteen ballistic missiles, and was built to be comparable to the US Polaris submarines.

Figure 31. The Charlie-I class nuclear-powered cruise missile submarine was the first Soviet submarine capable of firing its cruise missiles from a submerged position.

It could be fired at targets with ranges up to 35 nm away. Target acquisition and fire control data was obtained independently using the launch submarine's own sonar in passive and active modes. A capability also existed to receive target data via underwater communications from a surface ship, or from a different submarine acting as a forward observer. The Charlie-I class submarine with eight SS-N-7 cruise missiles could launch them from underwater while using the submarine's sonar or radio direction finder to provide sufficient target location information. However, the Charlie-I class submarines with their newer missile systems weren't yet totally replacing the older SS-N-3 armed Soviet submarines. These other systems were still being deployed, with some being modified to receive upgraded weapons systems, but they were still limited to firing only from the surface.

Strike tactics for the new Charlie-I class submarine armed with the submerged-launched SS-N-7 cruise missile were different from those used by the SS-N-3 units. The nuclear-powered Charlie had sufficient speed and endurance to intercept and trail a carrier task force under most circumstances. The maximum speed of US carriers was greater than the twenty-four knots of the Charlie-I class, but conventionally powered carriers and escorts had limited endurance at high speeds, and only nuclear-powered units could maintain high speeds over extended periods. The sonar sensors of the Charlie-I were capable of passively detecting a carrier within missile range, permitting targeting without external assistance. A Charlie-I could also launch all eight of its SS-N-7 missiles in rapid succession—a Soviet press article described the missiles as leaving the water like a flock of geese. (See Figure 33 on SS-N-7 cruise missile.)

The SS-N-7 missiles themselves were self guiding, freeing the submarine for evasive action after launch. Under some circumstances, a Charlie-I class unit might receive targeting assistance to supplement its onboard sensors.

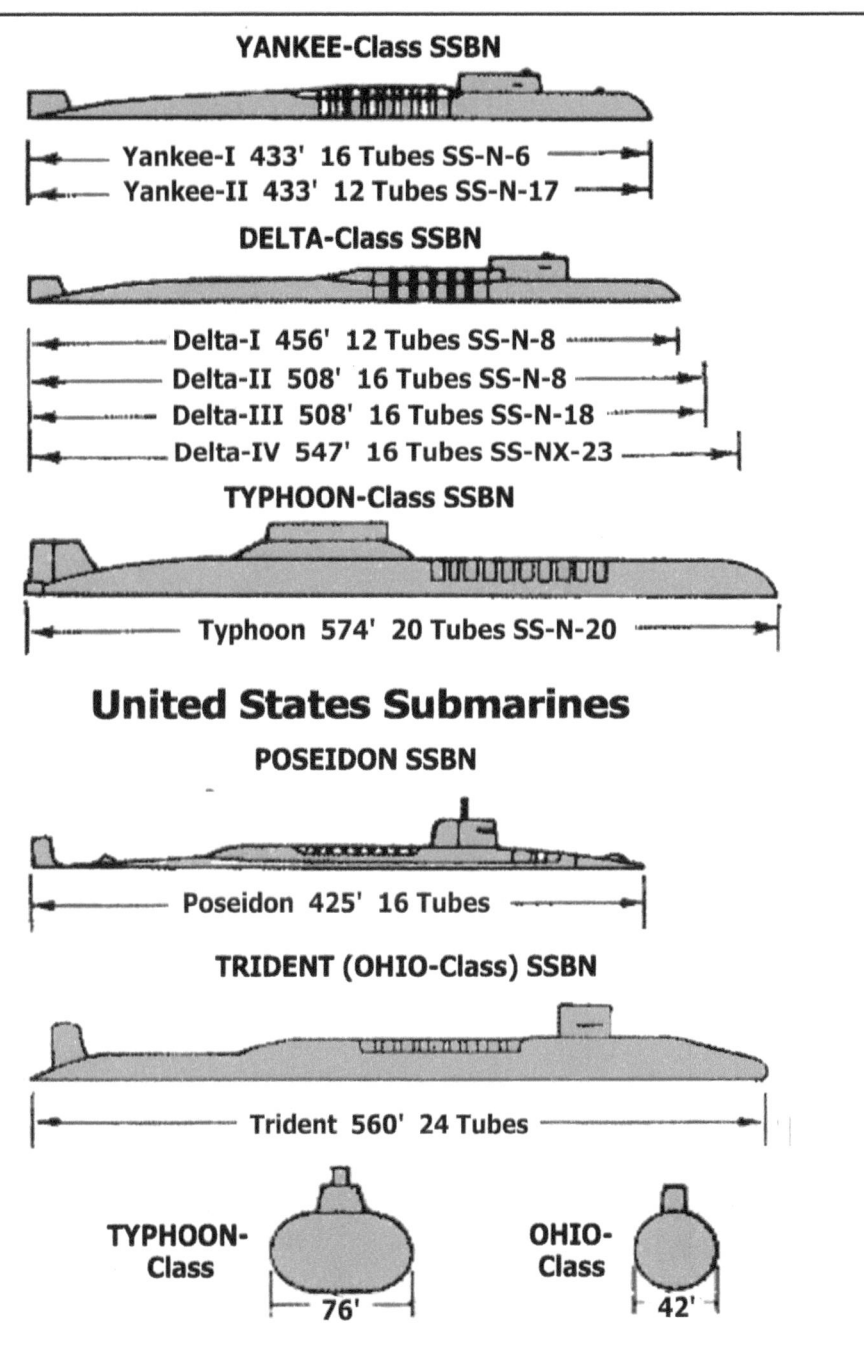

Figure 32. A size comparison between Soviet and United States classes of ballistic missile submarines.

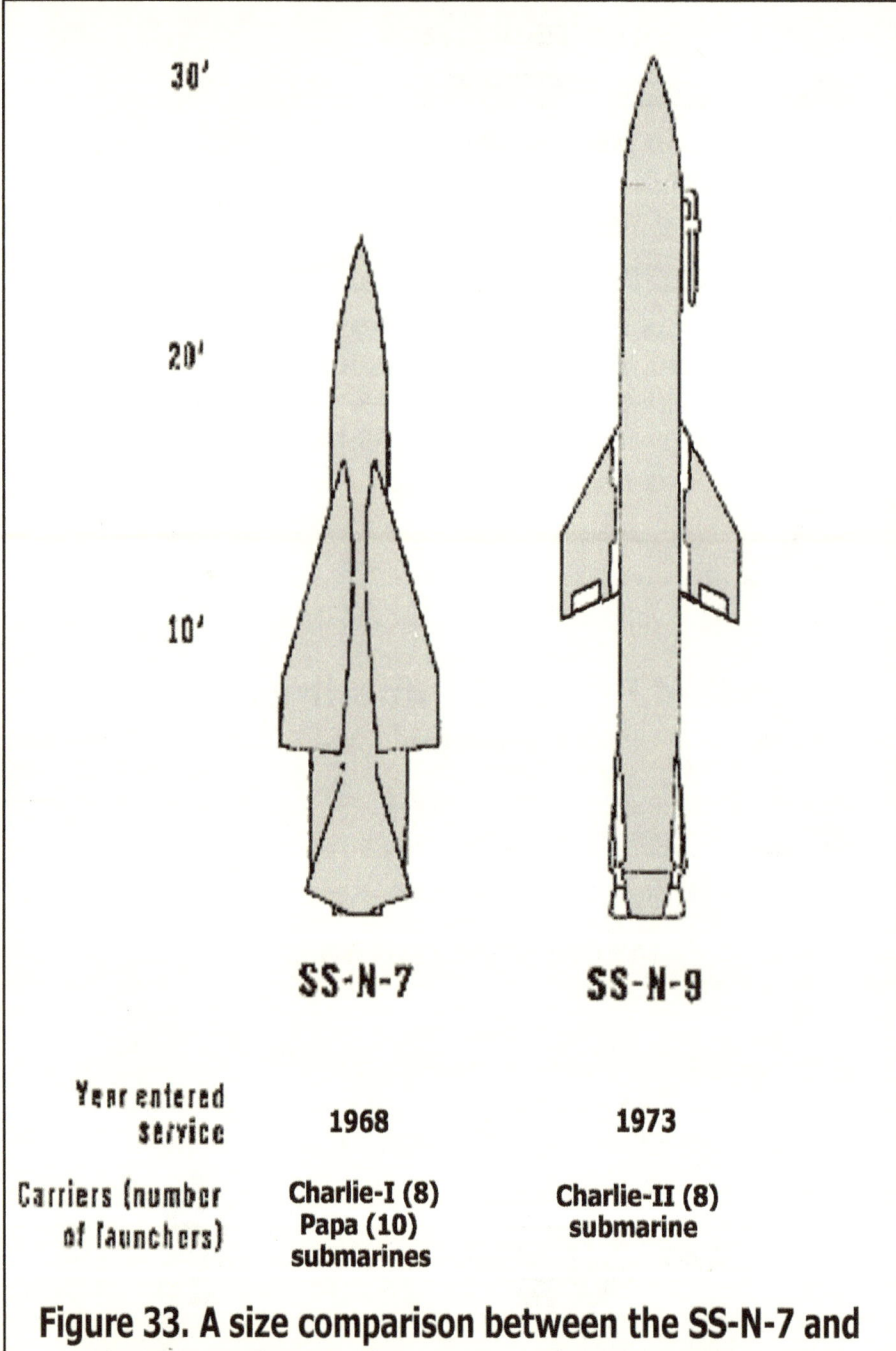

Figure 33. A size comparison between the SS-N-7 and SS-N-9 surface-to-air cruise missiles carried on Charlie and Papa classes of submarines.

Soviet operations in the Mediterranean included synchronizing activities in the vicinity of US carriers by using Charlie-I class submarines and Soviet surface combatants. In such cases, the surface combatants could pass their targeting information to the submarines via underwater communications systems. This tactic would be employed for preemptive strikes, but probably wasn't adequate enough under combat conditions. The basic concept for Charlie operations, therefore, emphasized independent attack. Besides the new Charlie-I class, another ASW submarine was released in 1968. These Bravo class submarines were built for testing new types of ASW weapons and crew training, along for use in coastal defense.

1968 Bravo Class

Although limited in range and endurance, the diesel-powered Bravo class SS (*Project 690 Kefal*) could respond quickly to coastal ASW alerts, and had the advantage of quieter submerged operations. The first Bravo class submarine entered service in 1968, and had a submerged speed of eighteen knots. They had an overall length of only 227 feet, and an operating depth limit of 985 feet. For armament, they each had one 21-inch torpedo tube and one 15.7-inch torpedo tube, with both at the bow. They carried up to six ASW torpedoes, and carried a crew of thirty-three. The ability of the Bravo diesel-powered submarine to get underway quickly, while also having quieter operations, created advantages in detecting outside enemy submarines approaching waters contiguous to the Soviet Union.

A diesel submarine like the Bravo class could get underway faster without time-consuming preparations, and provided quicker responses to a coastal ASW alert. In contrast, nuclear-powered submarines required several hours for a propulsion plant startup. Moreover, a diesel submarine while submerged and operating on its battery was inherently quieter than a nuclear powered submarine. They were also more compact, could operate in shallow waters and much closer to the shoreline. Their lack of speed and endurance, however—with a maximum of eighteen knots for only one hour—weighed against the use of the Bravo class as a covert trailing submarine against any enemies. The Bravo class became operational in 1968, and only four units were completed by 1970. They were considered a valuable class for safety and testing in ASW, being the only Soviet target submarines ever constructed.

A New Soviet Spy:

In late 1967 something curious happened—we had a US Navy warrant officer named John Walker suddenly enter our Soviet Embassy in Washington, D.C., and offer us a secret cipher card. We happily paid him a few thousand dollars for it—but more importantly, we also retained him on a salary of five hundred dollars a week as a Soviet spy. What he sold us proved to be quite important, but it was only half of the puzzle used in solving coded American messages. We also needed the decoding machines that went along with this card to be able to understand them. While this warrant officer wasn't able to supply us with a decoding machine, it did lead us into a later arrangement with North Korea.

On January 23rd, 1968, as the USS Pueblo was sailing along the North Korean coast, she was approached by a North Korean submarine chaser, and told to stand down. Other North Korean vessels also arrived and attempted to board the American naval ship, and eventually after a confrontation with shots being fired, she was seized and taken into a North Korean port.

On board was found a trove of cryptic information, including ten decoding machines and older cipher cards that allowed for the decoding of thousands of past secret messages. The crew was also interrogated for more information about these machines, and on decoding secret messages in general.

Another important development to come out later from this spy was information about the US acoustics program, and how our Soviet submarines were tracked and followed while underway. Since John Walker officially worked at the communications center for the US Atlantic submarine fleet, information about the SOSUS arrays and the detection of propeller noise from our Soviet submarines was easy enough for him to obtain.

This information became so valuable to us that it led to a complete re-assessment of our entire submarine program. Eventually this spy was apprehended by US authorities and sentenced to life in prison, but by then we had enough information to fully understand the gap that existed between our countries. We became determined to advance our submarines through various stealth methods to make them almost invisible from US detection.

A Fire In the Night:

On the night of September 8th, 1967, our November class nuclear submarine K-3 was on the 56th day of a long deployment, and was returning to base in the Norwegian Sea. It must be remembered that she was the first Soviet nuclear-powered submarine to become operational, and was the only nuclear sub to be designated Project 627, since all later subs of this class were identified as Project 627A.

She was also our first Soviet submarine to pass underneath the North Pole and to surface there, and was later given the honorary title Leninsky Komsomol. On that cold night in 1967, most of the crew were already asleep while submerged at fifty meters, with some of them likely dreaming about being back at base or ashore with their *girlfriends. Suddenly a report out of the first compartment arrived into the control room: "Fire in the forward bilges."*

Due to the fire Quarters was sounded, and the order was given to surface the submarine. Meanwhile, the fire spread rapidly and entered into the second compartment, where the overwhelming smoke and gases knocked out the fleeing crew. The bulkhead door leading to the third compartment was quickly sealed to contain the flames, as the automatic fire extinguisher system filled the first two compartments with carbon dioxide.

The submarine was then surfaced while the crew continued to assess the situation. An order was given to open the door to the second compartment to see if anyone could be saved. This allowed the carbon dioxide to flood the third compartment and knock out more crewmembers, who fell into unconsciousness. The third compartment was then sealed off for four days while the submarine returned to base. It total, thirty-nine members of the crew died inside the submarine from the fire and carbon dioxide gases.

An official Soviet investigation later determined that the leaking hydraulic system had probably started the fire, while the crew had behaved heroically to contain the fire. However, they also found that one sailor had died with a cigarette lighter next to him near where the fire had started, so this was most likely the source for the flame.

As was our Soviet custom, no honors were given for this careless accident even though many had put themselves at risk to save others.

However, an interesting development to this story occurred after the fall of the Soviet Union. It was found in a later inquiry that the cause of the fire was not due to a cigarette lighter, but rather was an improper gasket being placed into the hydraulic system (someone thought it would be safe to use the gasket out of a beer bottle).

Some Fishermen Help Out:

*I*n January of 1961 our Whiskey Twin-Cylinder submarine S-80 mysteriously disappeared while in the Northern Fleet during a training exercise, and had never returned to base. The long search conducted for S-80 in the Barents Sea used nearly fifty vessels and aircraft but eventually proved fruitless. For years, the location and circumstances of her disappearance were unknown, until a fishing boat that was trawling at around two-hundred meters in their normal fishing area suddenly snagged onto a large metallic object in 1968. This information was reported back to our Soviet fleet, so a search was conducted using a submersible bathyscaphe. While taking a dive to see the large obstacle, everything underwater remained in total darkness until a searchlight was eventually focused onto the bottom. To everyone's surprise, there in the watery grave was what we had been searching for years earlier, it was our lost sub S-80, with torn nets caught onto her tower and dangling down around the hull. The good news was she had finally been found, but what would come next?

After some discussions about the discovery within fleet headquarters, a Rear Admiral was placed in charge of the operation and given the task to raise this submarine. He then consulted with various experts for solutions, and after analyzing the possibilities, he had some engineers design a bridle that would latch over the sub and cradle her, then raise her to the surface. But such a thing had never been accomplished before, so it was an entirely new process. The submarine itself was sitting with a thirty degree list, but was resting evenly with no major damage observed to the outer hull. The rudder showed the sub has been turning to port with the diving planes in the surfacing position. Through planning, it was determined that everything necessary to raise the sub would have to be ready for the brief weather window of June to July of the following year *for a successful operation to be completed. But instead of rapidly developing and building the necessary equipment, everything got delayed past their deadlines. This caused the creation of a secondary plan which involved the use of a specially built salvage ship. She would be used to lower slings that would cradle the submarine and raise her to a depth of seventy meters, then tow her to sheltered waters where divers would place pontoons to complete the process.*

Mock up exercises using the salvage ship tested raising heavy objects from the depths, and it was found that shock absorbers were required to prevent the breaking of the slings. After some modifications and a few cuss words along the way, a final solution was found that worked, and it was completed just in the nick of time. The weather window was just opening during June of 1969, to where the final go-ahead was given to attempt the recovery. As work started, it became apparent that the submarine couldn't be raised to the original seventy meters depth, but instead it took nearly a month of trial and error to even raise the submarine five meters off of the sea floor, then shift her sixty meters away. The final towing began a few days later on the 10th of July, and on the 12th they lowered the submarine safely to the bottom of nearby Teriberskaya Bay. This fifty meters depth allowed divers to use pontoons to successfully raise the sub to the surface on the 24th of July. What a miracle!

Next, an investigative team analyzed the submarine and determined how she had sunk. On the night of 26 January, 1961, sub S-80 was at snorkel depth in heavy seas, and the weather above the surface was below freezing, a condition which created ice on any exposed objects. However, the de-icing system hadn't been properly turned on, and when a nearby vessel was suddenly spotted, they attempted a crash dive with the rudder over to port. A malfunction in the frozen valve closing the snorkel line caused the submarine to rapidly flood while losing her diesel engines, then she sank straight to the bottom. They also determined that the recovered sub was in no state to be repaired, and instead was sent to be cut up for scrap. However, the success of the salvage operation was to be commended. So in all it took nearly nine years for the mystery of S-80 to get resolved, all thanks to the torn nets of some local fishermen.

Soviet Submarine Fleet Conversion And Distribution:

During 1969 the conversion of older attack submarines was started when the cruise missile launch tubes were removed from earlier Echo-I submarines and newer sonars were added. Also, three of the six Zulu class units that were originally converted to fire ballistic missiles were reconverted back into torpedo attack submarines by removing their missile launch tubes. These submarine modifications were meant to improve Soviet ASW and interdiction capabilities.

The overall attack submarine force was assigned to four general fleet areas, but priority in assignment of the first line units was given to the two major sea areas–the Northern and Pacific Fleets. (See Figure 34 on Fleet HQ locations.) In these two main areas, Soviet submarines had access to the open sea. The Baltic and Black Sea areas required that Soviet submarines transit restricted waters which were under foreign control. All sixty-three nuclear-powered submarines available in 1969 were originally based in the Northern and Pacific fleets.

Of the sixty-six cruise missile units in the Soviet attack submarine force in 1969, thirty-five were stationed in the Northern Fleet and twenty-three were in the Pacific Fleet. Of the remaining eight cruise missile units–all of the old converted types–five were assigned to the Black Sea Fleet and three to the Baltic Fleet. Torpedo attack submarines were distributed among the Soviet fleet areas in a similar pattern. Of the 246 units, 106 (including seventeen nuclear-powered) were in the Northern Fleet, and eighty-seven (eight nuclear) were in the Pacific Fleet. The remaining fifty-three units (all diesel) were distributed almost evenly between the Baltic and Black Sea fleets.

Operations within the four fleet areas normally were in support of training and tactical development. Attack submarines in all the fleets were frequently involved in ASW exercises, torpedo firings, and the evaluation of new weapon systems and equipment. Baltic and Black Sea units also frequently participated in coastal defense, local interdiction, and local ASW exercises. The most distant operations originated from the Northern and Pacific Fleets, from their bases located in the Kola Gulf area in the North and the Petropavlovsk and Vladivostok areas in the Pacific. Submarines from the Baltic and Black Sea fleets deployed outside their fleet areas only occasionally.

Scope of Distant Submarine Operations:

During the 1960s, the Soviet attack submarine force departed from its pattern of short range operations and began to be deployed in the world's oceans in a deliberate program to gain experience in long range operations. By 1969, the number of identified out-of-area long range patrols by Soviet attack submarines had grown to 145 per year from less than forty in 1963. This amounted to an almost fourfold increase from 1963 to 1969, reflecting the Soviets' growing confidence in their ability to operate far away from home waters. The greatest changes occurred in the Mediterranean as a result of the reinforcement of the Soviet naval squadron following the 1967 Arab-Israeli War. The growth of distant operational activity in the Atlantic and Pacific were related to anti-Polaris operations, and the tracking of US carrier transits.

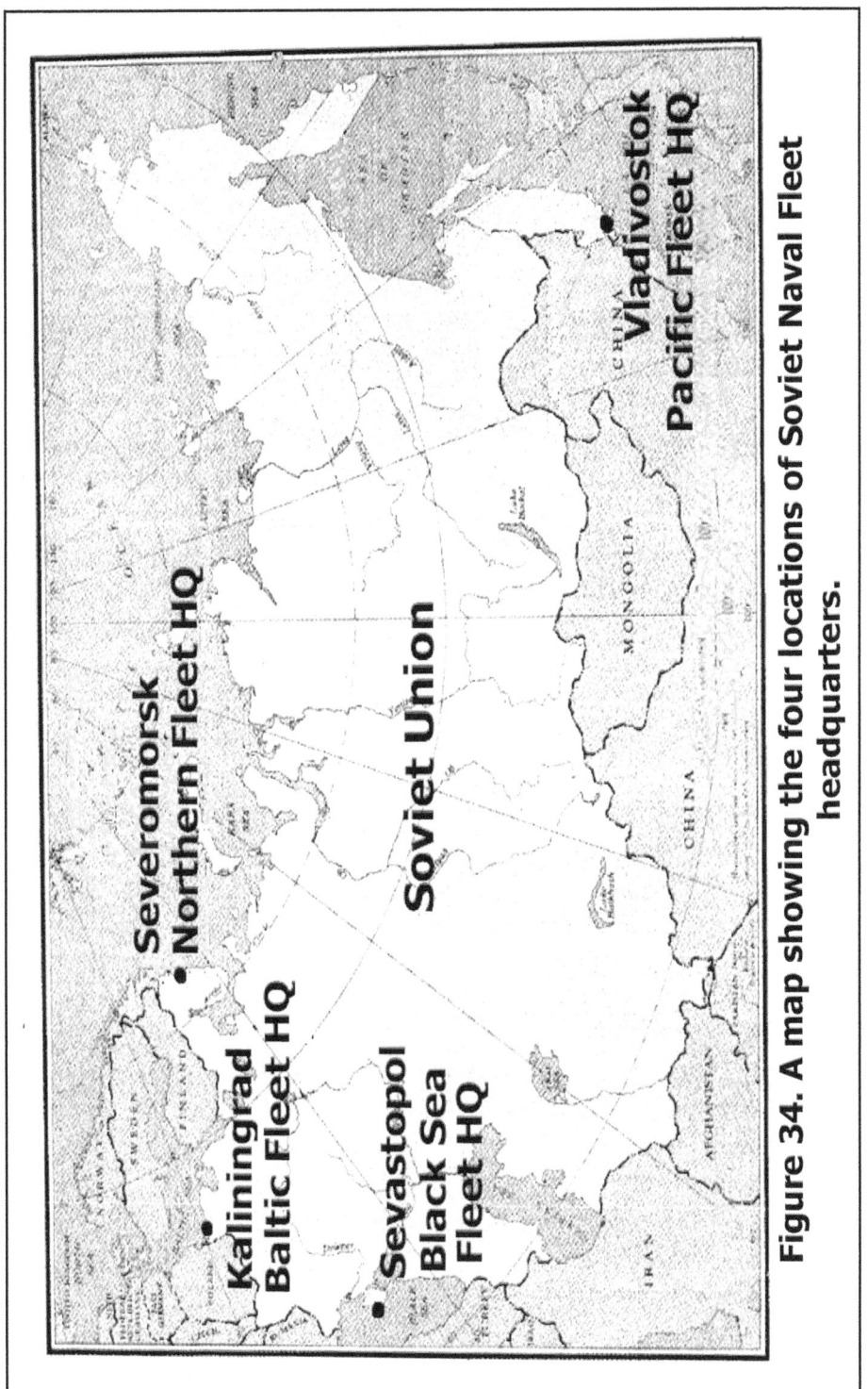

Figure 34. A map showing the four locations of Soviet Naval Fleet headquarters.

The character of Soviet attack submarine operations eventually grew more complex, more mission oriented, and more innovative. Soviet submarines during the early 1960s ventured out to the open ocean only while in the company of a rescue vessel. Later on, their attack submarines observed and stalked Western naval forces while patrolling unattended.

At the start of the 1960s, their attack submarine force was conducting under-ice transfers from the Northern Fleet to the Pacific Fleet. In 1966 the Soviet Union was able to conduct a submerged fleet transfer of two submarines from the Kola Gulf to Petropavlovsk and around South America—a distance of some 18,000 nm. In 1963, out-of-area patrols averaged about thirty days. In 1969, they averaged about seventy days.

To support this expanded scope of operations, the Soviets built a mobile support system with capabilities for replenishment and minor repairs when at sea. However, they didn't develop a system of foreign bases similar to the pattern of the United States, since to do so would be to condone what they had long condemned. The Soviets did, however, used joint facilities in Egypt—such as those at Alexandria and at Mersa Matruh—to provide limited submarine support. Soviet repair ships and tenders also serviced attack units in the Caribbean and the Mediterranean with little apparent reliance on shore facilities. (See Figures 35, 36 and 37.)

Soviet anchorages in international waters suitable for deployed submarine tenders were identified in the Indian Ocean, and in the Pacific Ocean near Guam. The Soviets also experimented with servicing submarines without mooring or anchoring. In 1967 a Soviet submarine tender on the high seas carried out a successful six-month submarine support operation near the Cape Verde Islands, off of Dakar in West Africa, while servicing both nuclear and diesel submarines.

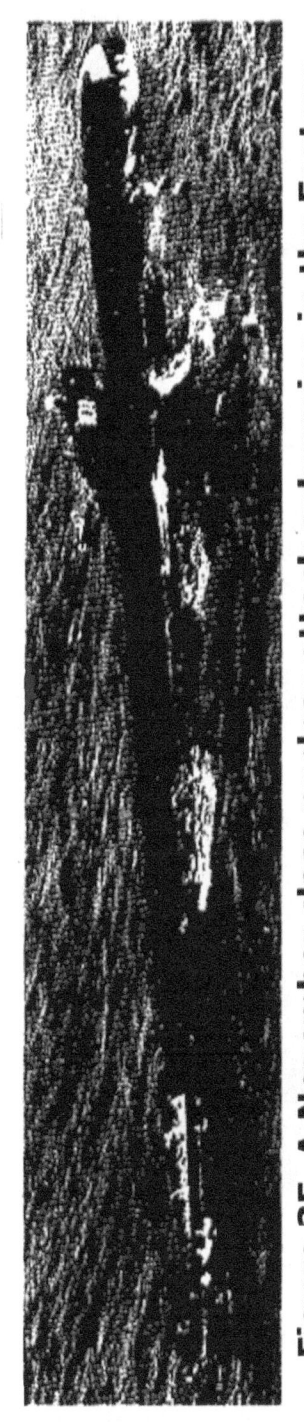

Figure 35. A November class nuclear attack submarine in the Eastern Mediterranean, during August of 1967.

Figure 36. A Foxtrot class diesel attack submarine coming alongside a Soviet Oiler for fuel off Tunisia during January of 1967.

In the Northern Fleet area, the Soviets experimented with moored buoy detection devices and had deployed them at strategic points. The earliest installation was near Russkaya Gavan, and it was operational in 1967.

Figure 37. An Echo-II class nuclear-powered submarine in the Gulf of Sidra off the Libyan coast during August of 1968. These submarines carried 250 nm range cruise missiles.

Other activities happened off of North Cape, where the Soviets installed a few of their moored buoys connected by cables to shore. This turned into the longest cable run to date by the Soviets–being over one hundred nautical miles. These moored buoy installations were meant to provide for the early warning of foreign submarine incursions into areas close to their naval bases in the Barents Sea area.

Pacific Fleet Surveillance:

A focal point for Soviet attack submarine operations at this time was expanded in the Pacific to include the vicinity of the Philippine Sea. Patrols had already been maintained in the region since 1965, and in 1968 the Soviets laid mooring buoys for surveillance in international waters 300 nm north of the US Polaris base in Guam. The moorage was well positioned for a tender to support anti-Polaris operations. In addition to the ASW activity, Soviet cruise missile submarines from the Pacific Fleet area and mid-ocean patrol zones reacted to US carrier transits to and from the west coast of the US by conducting simulated strikes. During wartime, a submarine defensive barrier would be established in the Kuril region, and at the three entrances to the Sea of Japan. This barrier deployment would serve the dual function of being both anti surface and for ASW defenses.

An alternative approach to obtaining broad area surveillance with a passive acoustic system involved the use of mobile sensors such as a towed array. The Soviets had used single hydrophones towed in seismic work in the Pacific, and seemingly understood the theories involved. A few Whiskey and Zulu class submarines in the Pacific were observed with winches and other suspected devices on their stern areas, but there was little belief that the Soviet Navy could successfully create a towed array system at a large enough scale. In addition, the Soviets were working since the early 1960s to develop a passive surveillance system to monitor the Arctic Ocean region under the ice cap. Some of this work was to support the under-ice operations of their Soviet nuclear submarines, and also involved underwater communications research. The Soviet Navy needed more data on the prevailing and expected sea ice conditions to ensure that their submarines were operating safety while underway in the region.

When planning for under-ice Arctic navigation, the Soviets considered ice features such as the frequency and extent of downward projections from the underside of the ice canopy, the distribution of thin ice areas through which their submarines could attempt to surface, and the possible locations of the outer pack edges where their submarines could remain surfaced during an emergency or to meet with surface ships or other submarines. Skylights were thin locations in the ice canopy less than one meter thick which appeared translucent from underneath. Soviet submariners considered Arctic locations to be friendly ice if they contained many such skylights large enough for surfacing along the projected track lines which they planned to follow. Equipment shipments and other evidence indicated that work was also being done on passive acoustic, under ice detection systems. Relatively simple systems could monitor significant areas within the Arctic Basin owing to the natural ducting effect occurring at the interface between the cold, stable water and the bottom of the ice cap itself. (See Figure 38 showing Foxtrot submarine in Arctic ice.)

Soviet Atlantic Fleet Patrols:

The Soviet Northern Fleet, with its many submarines and surveillance operations, was of prime intelligence interest to the United States government. This fleet was the primary source of ballistic missile submarines which posed an increasing threat to northern NATO territories, and to the continental United States.

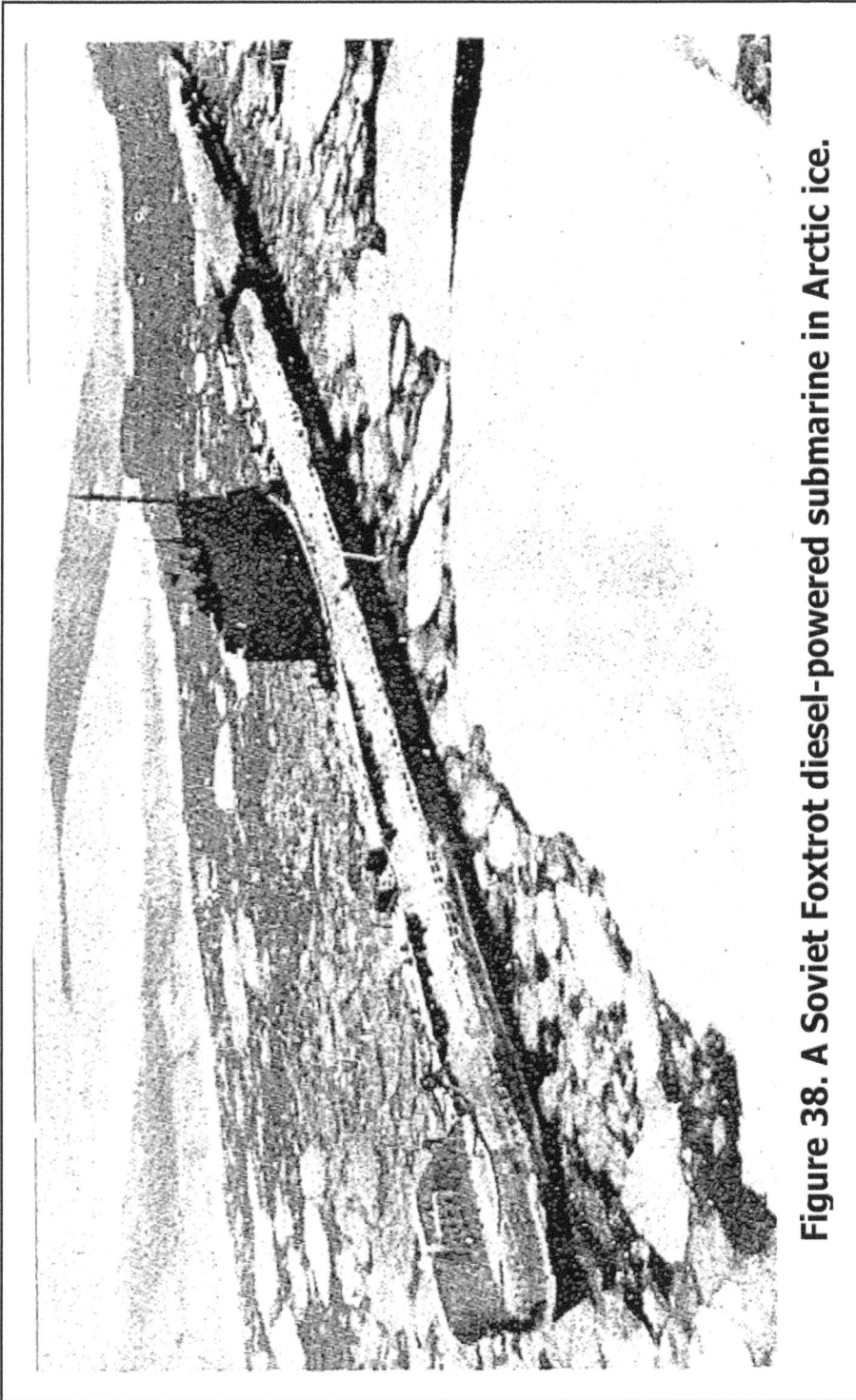

Figure 38. A Soviet Foxtrot diesel-powered submarine in Arctic ice.

The Northern Fleet's long range attack and cruise missile submarines also provided the Soviets with considerable naval firepower against any Free World merchant shipping and enemy naval surface units operating in the Norwegian Sea, the Atlantic and the Mediterranean. During this time the Northern Fleet was also providing the majority of the six to ten submarines regularly needed for patrolling the waters of the Mediterranean. Soviet attack submarine patrol areas were being established in the Norwegian Sea along the critical gap between Greenland, Iceland, and the United Kingdom—called the G-I-UK gap—and also by northern Norway. These patrol zones were occupied sporadically—usually in response to any US activity or in conjunction with their Soviet exercises. Submarines in these areas would be used during a crisis to track ships, or during a war to interdict US fleet movements.

Some of the Soviet exercise activities in the Norwegian Sea were linked to anti-Polaris operations. During a Soviet naval exercise held in 1970, nuclear and diesel-powered Soviet submarines engaged in ASW tactics against a Yankee-I class ballistic missile submarine which appeared to simulate a Polaris unit in the Norwegian Sea. Nearly continual operations west of the British Isles conducted by Baltic-based diesel submarines were related to the surveillance of US Polaris operations and British naval exercises. Many North Atlantic patrols were conducted by diesel-powered submarines, suggesting that they were primarily tasked for surveillance operations rather than the following of enemy contacts. The initial Victor-I class submarines were deployed to an operating area south of Iceland, a position which permitted surveillance of US submarine transits, and the delousing of their inbound and outbound Yankee class ballistic missile submarines. Delousing was a procedure in which the presence of a hostile trailing submarine was ascertained by using another trailing submarine for its detection and removal.

The Soviets eventually developed methods for protecting their Yankee class ballistic missile submarines from being trailed by Western nuclear submarines. The Soviets had begun conducting coordinated submarine transits within the Norwegian Sea that involved their Yankee class ballistic missile submarines proceeding to missile stations while accompanied by Charlie or Victor class submarines. Historically, the Soviet Navy was more inclined to operate submarines in companionship with other forces, including other submarines, than were Western navies. Two submarines operating together had made the first Soviet submarine fleet transfer around Cape Horn. Other groupings of six submarines had been transiting together from the Barents to the Mediterranean and back about once every six months.

Escorting Yankee class ballistic missile submarines also became an effective measure for discouraging or detecting potential covert enemy trailers. If the Soviet escort was far enough behind the Yankee class, the enemy trailer might interpose itself between the two, possibly subjecting itself to counter detection by the Soviet escort. Trailing the escort was an alternative approach for the enemy, but in that case contact with the Yankee class might be broken, sacrificing the initial mission objective. Once the presence of a trailing enemy submarine was disclosed, the Soviet escort could assist the Yankee class in attempting to evade through the use of countermeasures and with evasive tactics, or the Yankee class might instead try and outrun the enemy trailer by using its submerged speed advantage.

Mediterranean Area:

More than one-third of all distant Soviet submarine operations were done in the Mediterranean in an effort to cover NATO carrier operations, and to maintain a surveillance on Sixth Fleet movements and US Polaris operations. Most of the Soviet submarines assigned to the Mediterranean were based in the Northern Fleet. Often three cruise missile submarines, usually including one of the Charlie-I class, were maintained on station and were targeted against US carriers. Six Soviet torpedo attack submarines also deployed there on a six-month rotational basis for surveillance purposes. These submarines could form barriers in the Gibraltar and Sicilian Straits during any major crisis. The concentration of US Sixth Fleet units and Polaris submarines inside the confined Mediterranean waters offered many opportunities for Soviet surveillance and tracking operations. Their Mediterranean deployments were eventually extended by the placement of a Soviet repair ship at an anchorage in the Gulf of Sollum off of Egypt. This provided for replenishment services and for any needed maintenance to their diesel submarines. The USSR also took advantage of a loophole in the Montreux Convention of 1936—which disallowed submarine transits through Turkish straits except for needed repairs—by annually claiming repair activities on two of their submarines in the Baltic area and returning them to the Black Sea, while conducting patrols in the Mediterranean along the way.

Caribbean Area:

Soviet submarine operations in the Caribbean represented a further introduction of their attack submarine force into newer outside areas. In 1969, two Foxtrot class submarines entered Havana, the first such visits by any Soviet submarines. An ocean tug and two barges of a type associated with nuclear submarine maintenance were positioned in Cienfuegos, Cuba, in 1970. From late-1970 to mid-1971 a submarine tender visited Cuba three times—twice with an Echo-II class submarine, and once accompanied by a November class submarine. This Soviet interest in the Caribbean was for political and military reasons. Politically, all Soviet naval visits to the Caribbean were intended to acclimate the United States and Latin America to a Soviet presence there. The military value of a submarine support anchorage in Cienfuegos, Cuba was for provisioning an anchorage. As a peacetime facility it was used for their submarines engaged in surveillance operations against all US naval forces on the east coast, including US Polaris submarines, and for the emergency repair of any damaged or disabled submarines which were deployed off the US east coast. It was also meant as a forward contingency facility for which attack submarines could be deployed in advance of any crisis, and for eventual operations against any US east coast naval targets or Gulf of Mexico shipping.

Indian Ocean:

Since 1968, both nuclear and diesel-powered Soviet attack submarines also patrolled on occasion in the Indian Ocean. These submarine patrols were conducted largely for the familiarization of their crews into this new area of operation, and were also used as a hedge against any possible future large scale deployments of US or UK naval forces in the area. The Soviets had conducted extensive hydrographic operations in the Indian Ocean, which was another sign of their interest in future submarine operations there. If any NATO countries had increased their presence, particularly through the introduction of ballistic missile submarine patrols in the Indian Ocean, the level of Soviet attack submarine activity likely would have increased substantially.

Soviet Designs For Carrier Threat:

In addition to the growing interest in the anti-submarine warfare (ASW) mission, the Soviets continued to demonstrate their concern about US aircraft carriers. They viewed the aircraft carriers as a many-sided threat–a nuclear strike potential against the USSR itself, a threat to their Soviet naval forces, and also as an intervention force against them. The Charlie-I and Papa submarine classes represented a continuation of the cruise missile response to the US aircraft carriers, giving the Soviet attack submarine force a submerged-launched cruise missile capability along with the already established surface-launched one. In addition to this, they released the Alpha class a year later that focused on ASW capabilities.

1970 Papa Class

The experimental Papa class SSGN (*Project 661 Anchar*) was a large nuclear-powered submarine that had ten launch tubes which carried cruise missiles. Like the Charlie-I class, the Papa class cruise missile submarine represented continuing efforts to meet the US carrier threat while also having an ASW capability–primarily for self-protection. The Papa class was designed as an extremely fast attack submarine which recorded the fastest speed ever for a submerged submarine at 44.7 knots, and was the first Soviet unit to be built using a titanium hull. This submarine also carried ten SS-N-7 anti-ship cruise missiles which had a range of 35 nm, and could be launched while submerged for anti-carrier operations. The Papa class was longer than the Charlie-I class at 351 feet, and was considered a follow-up 2nd generation unit. For armament it had four 21-inch torpedo tubes at the bow, with room to carry up to twelve torpedoes. ASW torpedoes could be launched at depths down to 650 feet. It had an overall operating depth limit of 1310 feet, and carried a crew of seventy-five. The first and only Papa class submarine K-162 entered service in 1970, but no further units were ever constructed due to performance issues with the submarine's design and noise levels.

Figure 39. The nuclear-powered Alpha class was the fastest submarine ever built with speeds in excess of 40 knots. They had a shorter length of only 267 feet.

Figure 40. The four Delta classes of nuclear-powered submarines would form the backbone to the modern ballistic missile fleet of the Soviet Union.

1971 Alpha Class

The Alpha class SSN (*Project 705 Lira*) was the smallest of the new Soviet nuclear-powered submarines at only 267 feet long, and was a 3rd generation unit. (See Figure 39.) It represented a Soviet attempt to produce a deep diving, high speed submarine capable of operating at greater depths in order to enhance its ability to detect other submarines, and to evade enemy ASW weapons. The first submarine of this class was launched in Leningrad. It then spent about 18 months in a fitting out position between two barges used to support fitting out activities in connection with nuclear-powered attack submarines. Then in late 1970 this first submarine and its support barges departed the shipyard and were transferred through the inland waterway system to the Northern Fleet area, which is where the nuclear submarines built in the Baltic area often underwent their trials. The Alpha class had many experimental characteristics that differentiated it from those of other recent classes of submarines other than the Papa class. This led to many delays in its final fitting and testing. The first unit entered service in 1971, and had a remarkable submerged speed of 41 knots. For armament each one had six 21-inch torpedo tubes at the bow capable of using the latest torpedoes like the 53-65k or SET-65 versions. They could carry up to twenty torpedoes, and had an operating depth limit of 1310 feet. Only seven units entered service from 1971 to 1981, and each carried a crew of thirty-two. The Alpha class represented a further step in the Soviet search for a suitable ASW submarine.

With this latest Alpha class submarine, it meant that five newer attack classes were being produced by the Soviet Union–the Victor, Bravo, Charlie, Papa, and Alpha classes, with four of those being nuclear-powered. (See Figure 41 on submarine size comparison.)

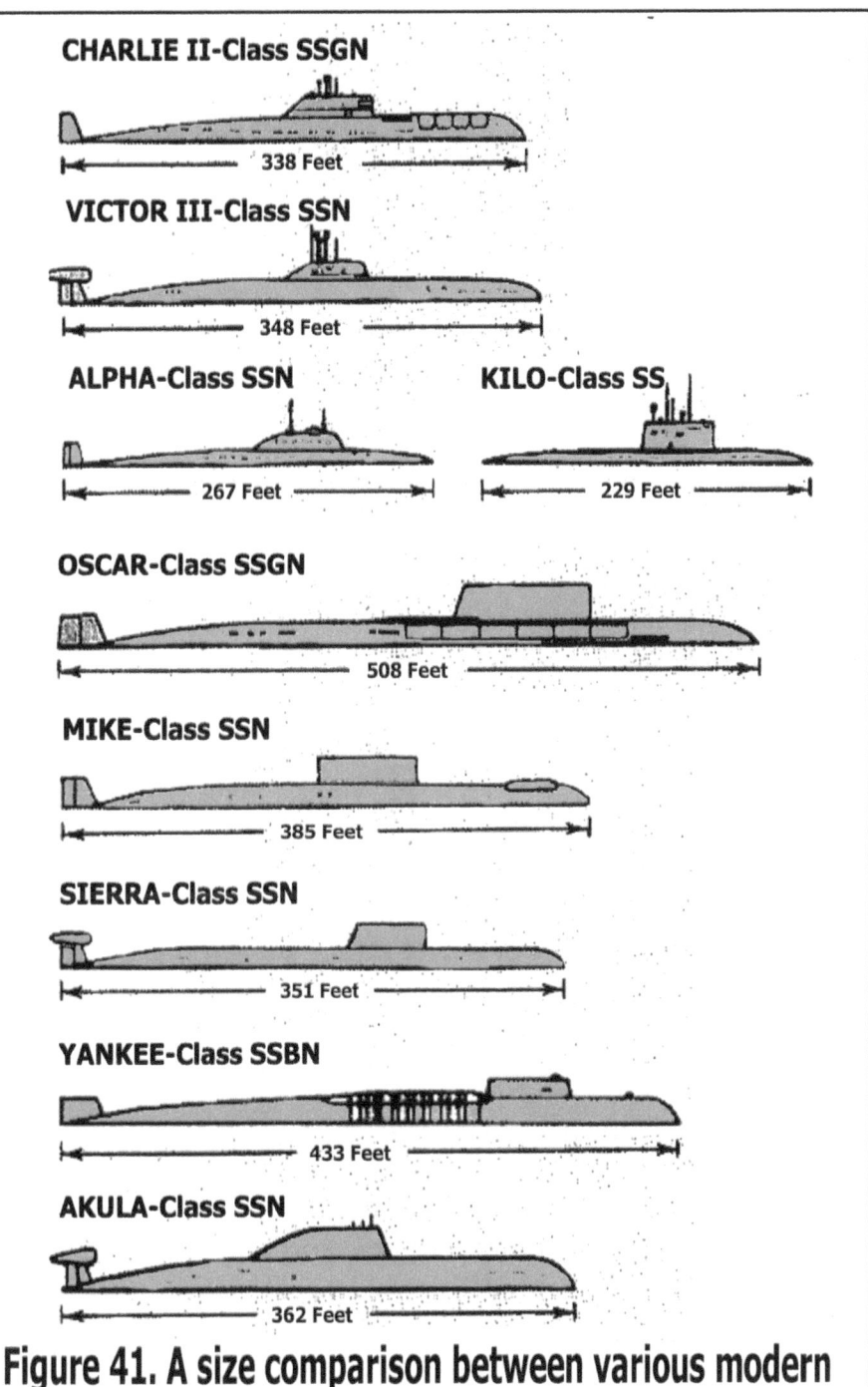

Figure 41. A size comparison between various modern Soviet submarine classes.

The Victor, Bravo, and Alpha classes were remarkably better designed for anti-submarine warfare (ASW) than the older classes of Soviet submarines. Still, half of the Soviet attack force remained too limited for use in interdicting sea lines of communication. There were only enough long range units to maintain a continuous interdiction force of about twenty-five submarines on station in the Atlantic and ten to fifteen in the Pacific. These numbers would increase however as the production of Soviet nuclear-powered submarines grew enough to expand their sea line and anti-carrier capabilities. (See Figure 42.)

Selected Years Mid-1955 to Mid-1975

	1955	1960	1965	1970	1975
Cruise missile and torpedo attack submarines	422	347	350	306	257
Nuclear		3	33	58	89
Long-range diesel	15	27	64	88	83
Medium-range diesel	123	212	208	150	82
Short-range diesel	284	105	45	10	3
Cruise missile launchers on submarines			217	384	468

Figure 42. The number of Soviet attack submarines by decade showing a decrease in short and medium-range diesel units, and an increase in the nuclear and long-range diesel units.

Another growing threat to the US carriers was the Soviet cruise missile submarines being deployed as preemption weapons. This type of submarine was seen operating in defensive barriers during exercises, and while shadowing US naval ships in the Mediterranean, Atlantic, and Pacific Oceans. The introduction of submerged launched cruise missiles in 1968 also further enhanced these abilities to effect a counter to any US carrier threats. (See Figure 43 on Soviet naval exercises.)

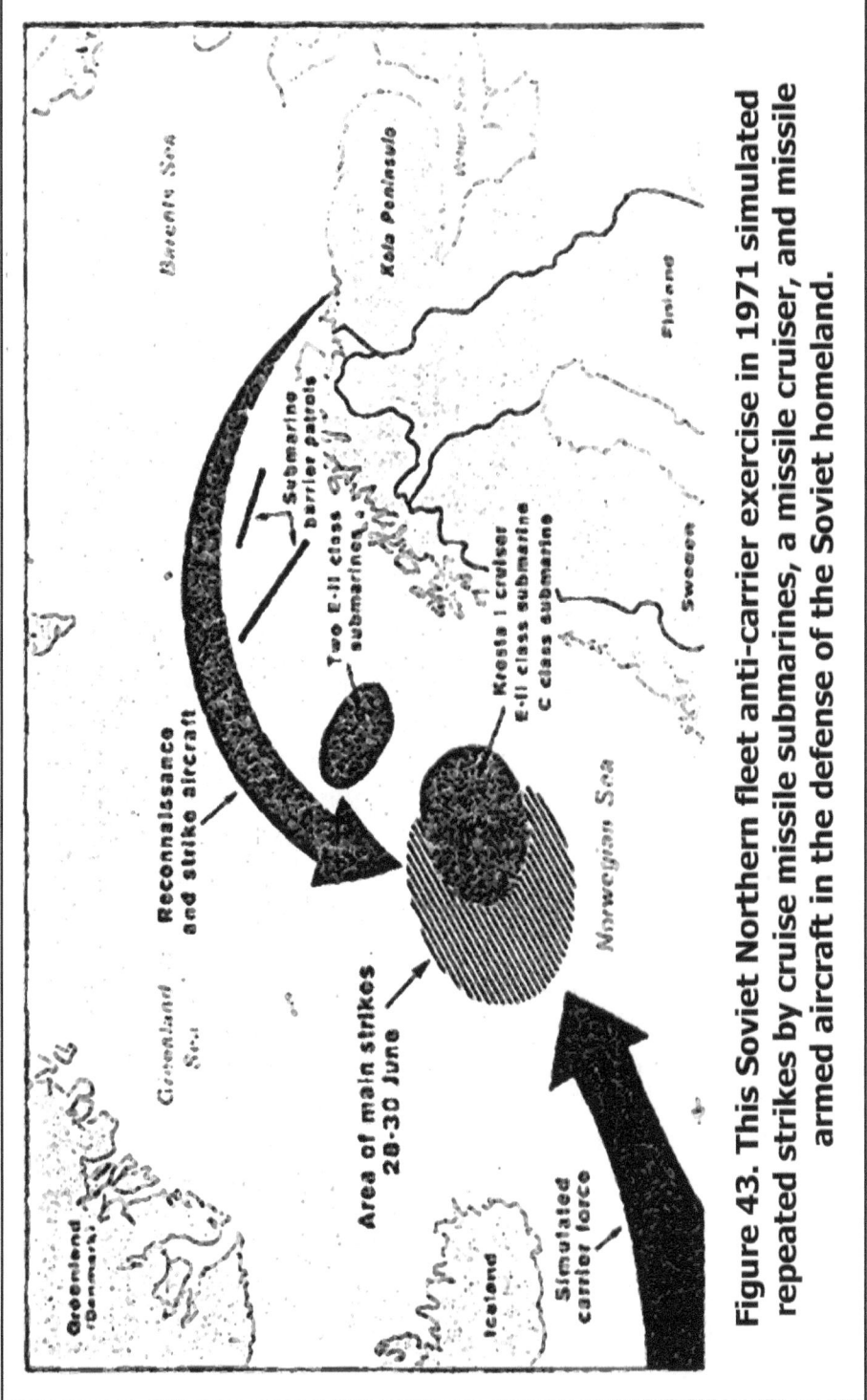

Figure 43. This Soviet Northern fleet anti-carrier exercise in 1971 simulated repeated strikes by cruise missile submarines, a missile cruiser, and missile armed aircraft in the defense of the Soviet homeland.

A Final Deployment:

*O*n *the 8th of April, 1970, our November class submarine K-8 was deployed on a training exercise in the Bay of Biscay while carrying nuclear weapons aboard. At 2230 during the evening they began rising to a depth of forty meters from 160 meters to make a routine communications check. They already had drank evening tea, and everything aboard seemed normal. But suddenly the warrant officer reported to control—"Fire in the sonar room!" Quarters was sounded for the crew, and everyone scrambled for damage control. A report came in from the seventh compartment. "We have an electrical fire in here!" The firefighting equipment available was fire extinguishers and an old air-foam system. Nothing could stop the fire in the control room itself, so the commander ordered the submarine to surface.*

With carbon monoxide gas smothering the crew, they were ordered out onto the main deck, which some could barely accomplish while gasping for air. The sea on the surface was relatively calm, however steam was seen coming off of the sub's hull back towards the stern. Then as a precaution the nuclear reactor inside needed to be shut down, so two engineers went in to activate the system, but they knew their chances of survival were low. Others began to descend and tried to get the remaining crew out of other compartments. Some had already succumbed to the smoke, but many scrambled out for air. Eventually, all the survivors huddled together outside on deck.

For the entire next day and night, they stayed outside on deck without any contact with outside help, but on the second day by chance a Bulgarian vessel noticed them just as the weather was getting rough. The ship came close by and asked if they needed any assistance through a megaphone. The reply was to radio Moscow. The ship stayed alongside until a reply came back, but by this time the fire had opened a small hole near the seventh compartment, and the submarine slowly began sinking by the stern. So the commander hastily ordered a group of forty-six crewmembers to go aboard the Bulgarian vessel to lighten the sub. Later than night two Soviet ships came to meet them and attempted to tow the submarine, but the lines they were using parted away instantly. Meanwhile, another ten of the crew were removed from the submarine and boarded one of the nearby Soviet tenders. Then as more attempts at towing happened, the sinking sub remained surfaced no more, and sank to the bottom of the bay with twenty-two crewmembers still inside her hull. She was the first Soviet nuclear-powered submarine that had been lost due to a sinking. Later, a monument was placed at the submarine base with little fanfare to commemorate those who had sacrificed for the rest of the crew, since Moscow didn't want to broadcast how dangerous being aboard a submarine was in those days—especially to any new recruits. Meanwhile, life went on for all the survivors of the sinking, as they were transferred to other submarines within our Soviet fleet.

1971 Anti-Submarine Warfare:

After the introduction of the US nuclear-powered ballistic missile submarines, the dimensions of the ASW problem for the Soviet Union was radically altered. Those US nuclear submarines—because of their speed, endurance, and their capability to remain completely submerged for longer periods—were much harder to find and track than were the older US submarines. Also, the US ballistic missile submarines didn't need to approach any hostile forces to carry out their mission, and instead would evade them on purpose. More importantly, the US ballistic missile submarines had a far greater destructive potential than earlier submarines—a factor which drastically altered Soviet

ASW requirements. In past wars, any major reduction in damage was an acceptable goal, but in a nuclear war failure to destroy every ballistic missile submarine—while leaving even a few—could still mean a nuclear catastrophe. Only one US Poseidon submarine, for example, was capable of delivering approximately 160 nuclear warheads. The consequences of allowing even one such submarine to launch its missiles against the Soviet Union could be catastrophic.

During 1971 the Soviet Navy still had a total of about 340 submarines in service, which remained the largest submarine fleet in the world. About fifty-five of those had a strategic strike mission, while the remainder—some 285 attack submarines—were the principal force for strategic defense against the US Polaris submarines, for countering aircraft carriers, and for interdicting sea lines of communication. The Soviet attack submarine force was an important contributor to their own ocean surveillance system. Their first line base was also increasing through a large construction program, and as obsolete submarines were retired from service.

The beginnings to Soviet open ocean anti-submarine warfare (ASW) also coincided with the post-World War Two venturing of the Soviet Navy out onto the high seas from coastal areas. The development of ASW defenses for their fleets at sea eventually would occupy much of the Soviet effort since that time. The emergence of US attack submarines that were nuclear-powered, moreover, increased the Soviets long-standing concern for the security of their coastal areas and inter-coastal shipping. Consequently, they initiated efforts to develop ASW defenses in coastal areas, as well as for the open ocean. The Soviet Navy had increasingly exposed its forces for political and military recognition in distant areas such as the Caribbean, the Mediterranean, and the Indian Ocean. The credibility of these forces as instruments of Soviet foreign policy and their viability in hostile circumstances were dependent on their defensive capabilities. The Soviets considered cruise missile armaments on most of their surface forces to be adequate against the surface threat. But experience taught them to be less than complacent about their abilities to deal with the US attack submarines. They took measures to bolster their defenses against them in particularly vulnerable areas, such as in the Mediterranean, through the use of surface, air, and submarine barrier forces.

The Soviets were also concerned that any concentrated areas of naval and maritime activity along their Soviet coastline would be particularly appealing to US attack submarines during a war. These areas were also sensitive in peacetime as Soviet forces conducted naval exercises and while employing advanced systems testing. The Soviets regarded the US attack submarines that were nuclear-powered as the greatest threat to their own fleet of ballistic missile submarines. They had concluded that they would expect to confront Western submarine barriers in areas on their routes from bases out to the open seas. The Soviets had learned US methods for trailing and escorting ballistic missile submarines. These observations eventually led them to escorting some of their Yankee class missile submarines while using their own attack submarines as similar trailing defenses whenever possible. Beyond these submarine tactics there were new strategies also being realized in their anti-carrier capabilities with the introduction of a new super torpedo. This version was first carried aboard the Victor-II class submarines, and was meant for sinking US aircraft carriers.

1972 Victor-II Class

The Victor-II class SSN (*Project 671RT Syomga*) attack submarine was an improved anti-carrier version of the earlier Victor-I class which included carrying a new super torpedo. Since the regular torpedoes used in 21-inch tubes required many hits to sink a single aircraft carrier, a more powerful version was created for a 25.6-inch diameter torpedo tube. These were capable of sinking a carrier with a single strike. These 65-73 "super torpedoes" were also fifty percent longer, and had nuclear warheads with an explosive force of nearly one ton of TNT. Soviet testing had earlier concluded that their nuclear warheads were a perfect match to fit into these for this explosive potential. During construction, the Victor-II torpedo compartment was lengthened to accommodate these longer torpedoes. They could be launched from any depth, and ran at an impressive fifty knots. The only drawback was they remained unguided. There were seven Victor-II submarines produced from 1972 to 1978, and each had an overall length of 334 feet. Their operating depth limit was 1310 feet. For armament each had four 21-inch torpedo tubes and two 25.6-inch torpedo tubes, all at the bow. They could carry up to six 65-73 super torpedoes, and eighteen regular torpedoes. Each required a crew of sixty-eight.

A Long Ordeal:

*O*n *the 24th of February, 1972, our Hotel class nuclear submarine K-19 (now nicknamed "Hiroshima" by her crew) was again returning from a long deployment back to base. It was a half hour before reveille at a depth of 120 meters when a fire suddenly flashed into the ninth compartment. This was the sleeping quarters area and the watch got everyone awake, then reported the fire to the control room. The ring of damage control quarters alerted everyone. The speed of the ensuing hydraulics fire had isolated the tenth compartment—which was the aft torpedo room—from everyone else, while an attempt to contact them by phone was eventually made. They reported back that the forward bulkhead was already smoldering, however the VPL airfoam system hadn't stopped the fire in ninth compartment.*

Meanwhile, the order was given to surface since some in the crew were badly gasping for air, while others had already succumbed to the gases. Desperately these crewmembers began to get dragged to forward compartments to see if they could be resuscitated. Once the sub had surfaced, many were told to go up on deck into the sail, even though a raging storm was upon them. But back aft in the tenth compartment some were still isolated, now with twelve men there alive and accounted for again by using a telephone. However, the ninth and eighth compartments continued burning, while the seventh and sixth were full of hot gasses—so there was no possible way to rescue those in the tenth compartment at this time, although constant contact by telephone was attempted. Then, after several hours, they reported having used up their emergency breathing gear in tenth compartment. The chances for them to survive the fire now seemed bleak.

Unfortunately due to the isolated location of the submarine and being far from any navy bases, it took two days for the first ship to respond to their emergency calls. Then a cargo ship finally approached, and they attempted to pass a towline, but two of the sub's crew fell into the bucking waters while attempting to connect to it, and no other attempts could be made. Then a short while later a large Soviet ASW ship approached. They had aboard a helicopter that was able to bring supplies to the stricken sub, and lowered them to the surprised crew using a cable. Dry clothing, lanterns, some food and breathing gear came inside. They even included hot coffee. It was also decided that the helicopter would start retrieving some of the crew from the sub, so they began to lift them away one-by-one and take them to the ASW ship. Then another vessel, a nearby rescue tug, also began to take crewmembers, but had them jump into the cold ocean and swim after clipping on a rescue line. This continued until only eighteen seamen–who were to remain aboard for salvage control– were left on the sub.

It must be emphasized that all of this was occurring during the month of February, one of the coldest months at sea in the North Atlantic by Newfoundland. Wearing wet clothes for days and attempting to perform emergency duties proved very tiring and hypothermic in the bitter coldness. But no one bothered to complain, as they had to save the twelve men left trapped aboard their submarine. So after many dangerous attempts to attach a tow cable, and many days later while having a replacement crew from a nearby submarine for assistance, K-19 began her trip back to the nearest base, at which time they were finally able to open the tenth compartment. By some miracle, those twelve souls had stayed alive–while in total darkness and only with emergency rations–for a total of three remarkable weeks. This rescue had happened on March 18th, and while a few of them couldn't even walk anymore, they had none-the-less survived! All twelve of them left the submarine to a hero's welcome, receiving warm food and much needed care ashore. But the end result was that the fire had killed twenty-eight submariners who ended up buried at sea, with two later succumbing while on the way home. Also to be remembered were those who died bravely at their stations, holding out to save others until their very last breath.

Soviet Capabilities for Submarine Detection:

The Soviets had recognized that they must develop systems and tactics to solve each of the three elemental tasks needed for successful anti-submarine warfare–which was the detection, localization, and the destruction of an enemy submarine. Any possible detection had become more complex with the advent of ballistic missile submarines, with the chief problem being the vast ocean areas which must be searched for them. The more traditional problems of coastal ASW and fleet defense required only searching in restricted areas along coastlines or around deployed forces. But the detection system developed for such limited area searches and for localized targets wasn't adequate for searching much larger open areas of the ocean.

Therefore, a surveillance system capable of conducting open ocean searches seemed a necessity for combating ballistic missile submarines in any strategy which didn't rely on submarine trailing tactics. It could also be a significant aid for other forms of ASW. For example, an ocean surveillance system could warn deployed forces or coastal defensive units of any approaching hostile submarines. Ocean surveillance systems could conceivably be attached to the seabed, located in satellites, positioned ashore, or be carried by conventional naval forces. Such phenomena as acoustics, magnetics, wake turbulence, communications interception, and infrared could possibly become the basis for an ocean-wide detection system. However, the Soviets never produced any mobile or fixed detection devices useful for the long-range detection of US submarines. The Soviet sensors aboard ships and aircraft had short-range detection only and were designed for localized or small-area searches, while Soviet fixed acoustic detection devices in use were passive systems used for shorter ranges as well.

Instead, the Soviet production programs, tactics, and training concentrated chiefly on the localization phase of ASW. Once a submarine had been detected by an ASW force, its position and movements had to be determined with sufficient accuracy to launch a weapon. One of the greatest obstacles to the development of effective ASW sensors was the effect of environmental conditions which limited the performance of the sensor in locating a submarine. Sonar, the most widely used ASW sensor, was affected by water temperatures and salinity, the depth of the target, the topography of the ocean floor, and other factors. The uncertainties involved in depending on a single type of sensor led both the US and the USSR to develop other shorter range ASW sensors, such as magnetic detection systems, that weren't as susceptible to these particular environmental conditions.

Sonar could detect the presence of a submarine either passively by detecting the sound generated by the submarine, or actively by transmitting a sound pulse and detecting its return echo. Surface ships ordinarily utilized active sonar, but submarines could employ either mode effectively.

Sonar performance depended on its ability to discriminate any submarine noise or returning echoes from the sonar's electrical noise, the platform's noise, and the ambient noise of the sea. In the active mode, sonar was also degraded by sound energy reflecting from the ocean's surface and from the ocean bottom, and by the scattering and absorption of sound energy into the ocean itself.

The adverse effects of some natural phenomena could be reduced by using sonar which operated at lower frequencies, since a lower frequency signal resulted in less absorption of sound from the ocean. A larger acoustic array was needed, however, to obtain any directional accuracy at lower frequencies.

Magnetic anomaly detection (MAD) devices, the second most widely used ASW sensors, could measure disturbances in the earth's magnetic field generated by a submarine. MAD sensors were usually installed only aboard aircraft because surface ships and submarines created disturbances in the earth's magnetic field which would interfere with a MAD system. Radar, optical, infrared, or radio direction finding equipment could also be used by ships and aircraft to detect submarines at or near the ocean's surface.

Soviet submarine sonars up to this point had undergone three identifiable stages of development. The first postwar Soviet sonars, installed on some Whiskey, Quebec and Zulu class submarines during the first phase, were relatively ineffective as their power levels were lower and their frequencies were too high. Soviet submarines of the Juliett, Hotel, Echo, November, and Foxtrot classes were outfitted with the second generation of sonars featuring lower frequencies and greater power. Available evidence suggested that second generation sonars achieved passive detection ranges less than half those of US units. Soviet submarines during the third phase—with the Charlie, Victor, Yankee, and Papa classes—were equipped with powerful active sonars of the third generation. Although a number of improvements were incorporated into this generation of sonars, experience of US forces indicated that Soviet passive detection ranges were still only half compared to those of US nuclear submarines. Much of this difference was mainly due to the noise interference being generated by the Soviet submarines themselves.

The Soviets had done much theoretical work on low-frequency sound propagation, and had conducted at-sea propagation experiments in the appropriate frequency regions. There were, however, five factors which limited the Soviets potential for exploiting acoustic techniques to detect all US submarines. One main limitation was a fundamental geographic problem. Long-range, passive acoustic detection systems worked only in deep water. Except for certain areas in the Pacific, such regions were at great distances away from the Soviet coastline. Moreover, the Soviets didn't have allies which were strategically located for the emplacement of such systems. Complementary to the geographic problem was an apparent Soviet deficiency in cable technology. The Soviets were several years behind the US in low-impedance underwater cable technology. To build out a SOSUS-like detection system they would have needed cable runs of over one-thousand miles long, or to develop a satellite readout capability. A third constraint was the apparent Soviet lack of a low-frequency signal processing capacity. Another factor that hindered the Soviets in perfecting detection systems was their inclination for using rigid hydrophone arrays in their acoustical systems, when flexible arrays were a practical necessity for creating any type of long-range detection system similar to SOSUS.

The quietness of US nuclear submarines was perhaps the most difficult problem the Soviets were encountering in ASW. Although the US SOSUS system could detect Soviet submarines fairly reliably, those submarines were an order of magnitude noisier than the modern US ballistic missile submarines were. By contrast, since SOSUS couldn't reliably detect the location of US submarines, the Soviets would have needed a system that went beyond the capabilities of SOSUS. The Soviets did however develop shorter range, passive acoustic detection devices which they were using for ports and harbors. A few passive acoustic systems were employed in the Pacific to monitor areas within straits and at entrances to ports. These were all in relatively shallow water and were of a limited range only.

A Soviet alternative to having a large ocean surveillance network like SOSUS was to use their attack submarines to gain contact on enemy submarines in a narrow strait or base area, and then to trail them. Their submarines, however, still didn't have the ability for the continuous trailing of US ballistic missile submarines. Although the speed and active sonar capabilities of the Victor class were adequate for the trailing of non-evading US submarines, the requirements inherent in trailing escorted SSBNs or SSBNs employing tactical counter-measures exceeded the potential of the Victor class. Even if the Soviets believed that the Victor class was adequate for trailing them, a minimum of one-hundred submarines would have been needed to maintain a force sufficient for the detection and trailing of the total US Polaris force. But the Soviets only had nine Victor class units operating at this time, and were building new ones at the rate of only two per year. Any Soviet plans to trail more than one Polaris submarine actively would also need to account for the defensive reaction used by the US Navy. Not only would assisting forces be sent to the aid of any trailed US submarines, but those deployed would have used delousing to intercept and out-maneuver any trailing Soviet submarines.

Soviet Capabilities for Destruction:

Anti-submarine Warfare (ASW) weapons in use by the Soviet Navy consisted of acoustic homing torpedoes, standard depth charges, and small rocket-propelled charges fired in salvos from any detecting surface ships. In addition to these ASW weapons, the Soviets had mines which also had ASW applications. The Soviets had produced three types of nuclear submarines since the late 1950s—torpedo attack, cruise missile attack, and ballistic missile submarines. These types of subs were built in two consecutive generations. During the first generation, the cruise missile attack submarine program was predominant in terms of units produced. Cruise missile submarines were designed primarily for attacking surface ships. During the production of the second generation, the Soviets concentrated more on ballistic missile submarine construction. According to the Soviets, nuclear-powered torpedo attack submarines such as the Victor class were the appropriate submarines for ASW. And since 1967, these were being produced at a constant rate of about two submarines per year.

The Main Naval Staff in Moscow was ultimately responsible for managing all of the Soviet submarine operations, including ASW. The four fleet commanders (Pacific, Northern, Baltic, and Black Sea) were directly responsible for anti-carrier warfare, ASW, and all other operations in their area of responsibility, except for SSBN operations. The fleets had no deputy commanders specifically for operational control of ASW forces such as the Atlantic and Pacific fleets of the United States. The Soviet naval command system was characterized by the highly-centralized operational control of their ships and submarines at sea, and was entrusted to the Main Naval Staff in Moscow. The chief impetus for centralization came from the need for positive control of nuclear weapons and naval forces in close proximity to Western naval forces on the high seas. The Main Naval Staff had the capability for direct control of Soviet ships and submarines in the Mediterranean and Norwegian Seas, and in the North Atlantic and Indian Ocean. The main Naval Staff relied on Pacific Fleet headquarters in Vladivostok for operational control of all naval forces operating in the Pacific. The Soviets developed both short and long range communications systems for their submarine fleets, including for their latest submarine, an improved Charlie class unit.

1973 Charlie-II Class

The Charlie-II cruise missile class SSGN (*Project 670M Skat-M*) was an improved anti-ship and ASW version of the earlier Charlie-I class. During construction, a twenty-six foot insert was placed into the hull that incorporated advanced electronics for controlling eight SS-N-9 Siren cruise missiles. The SS-N-9 Siren (*P-120 Malakhit*) resembled the SS-N-3 Shaddock but was operationally superior to it due to its lower flight path and faster speed. Its size allowed the missile to fly beyond the radar horizon, out to a distance of 60 nm at a maximum speed of Mach 1.4. A forward target relay could be used, and it was submerged launched from depths of 165 feet. It first went operational on the Charlie-II class submarine in 1973. This version—like the earlier Charlie-I– had a single nuclear reactor and a single propeller shaft which reduced their top speed. They were also the first Soviet submarines to obtain targeting assistance using surveillance satellites. The first of six Charlie-II units became operational starting in 1973, and they had an overall length of 338 feet. For additional armament they had six 21-inch torpedo tubes at the bow, with room to carry up to fourteen ASW torpedoes. They had an operating depth limit of 985 feet, and each carried a crew of one-hundred. Since the Charlie-II class only had a top speed of 24 knots while submerged, this was considered too slow for a nuclear-powered submarine, so they were eventually phased out. Besides the new Charlie-II class, a ballistic missile submarine was also introduced In 1973, the important Delta-I class.

1973 Delta-I Class

The Delta-I class SSBN (*Project 667B Murena*) was a 2nd generation nuclear-powered ballistic missile submarine and was created as an extension of Yankee class technology. When the first Delta-I submarine was launched in 1973, construction on the final Yankee-I submarine was being completed. The Delta submarines were built in four different classes, with the first Delta-I class carrying twelve SS-N-8 Sawfly (*R-29*) ballistic missiles which were launched from an underwater depth of 180 feet. (See Figure 40 on page 99.) All versions were constructed with a double hull. The Delta-Is started entering service in 1973 and had a submerged speed of 25 knots. They included an overall length of 456 feet. For additional armament they had four 21-inch torpedo tubes and two 15.7-inch torpedo tubes, all at the bow, with room to carry up to sixteen ASW torpedoes. They had an operating depth limit of 1310 feet. Eighteen units entered service from 1973 to 1977, and each carried a crew of 120. These Delta-I submarines were meant to bypass the US SOSUS detection system by being able to launch their ballistic missiles away from its detection areas. The Delta-II class (*Project 667BD Murena-M*) was a lengthened version of the Delta-I at 508 feet that allowed for fourteen SS-N-8 Sawfly ballistic missiles. It had improved quieting measures through the use of shock absorbers under the steam turbines, along with rubber insulation for piping and special acoustic coatings on the hull. This version started entering service in 1975.

A Stolen Submarine:

*T*he Soviet National Anthem played aboard a United States ship that was constructed to raise one of our lost Soviet submarines from great depths. This had occurred in August of 1974, after the recovery of the remains and the stealing of our technology right out from under us. The story is a long one, and the end result was six of our Soviet seamen were buried at sea by the CIA of the US government, under the guise of a commercial mining ship, the MV Glomar Explorer.

The submarine they raised portions of was K-129, which had left port over six years earlier on the cold morning of February 24th, 1968, off the Kamchatka peninsula. Contact with her was made after a first dive, and all had seemed well. But when the sub failed to report back after reaching the 180th meridian, it raised suspicions within fleet headquarters. Then another communications check was missed, and news broke about the U.S. submarine Swordfish arriving in Japan with upper damage to her sail structure. Had she had a collision with our missing submarine? Some at Soviet fleet headquarters suspected this was the case, so a search was started that traced back to where K-129 might have first lost contact with the fleet. Nothing related to the missing submarine could be found. Then the search was expanded again and ultimately covered over a million square miles using many types of vessels and aircraft, but again nothing was found relating to our lost submarine. So the search was wound down and she was considered lost at sea.

Meanwhile, the United States had used their impressive underwater sound surveillance system called SOSUS to pick up the sound of an underwater explosion in the area at the time of the loss, and this led them to the location of our lost sub by using search grids to find her. It was also speculated they already knew an approximate location since their own sub has made contact during a collision. In any event, they used this information to develop a plan to raise the entire submarine they found from a great depth of over 16,000 feet–which was nearly 3 miles deep. The CIA built a ship entirely for this purpose, and used a large claw that was set over our submarine and clamped around the hull, then used hydraulics to slowly lift her from the bottom. Unfortunately for them a portion of the submarine broke away on the way up, while the rest was placed into the waiting ship above as a prize. Then as they conducted inspections and assessed what was inside, the dead seamen they found were removed and buried at sea. This was even recorded to prove it had all happened according to Soviet customs. But the story of this recovery and the covert manner in which it was carried out infuriated and amazed many at our fleet headquarters. How could it be done? Why didn't we do it ourselves? Instead we covered up the loss like so many other submarine accidents that happened during the Cold War, while not wanting to acknowledge the actual retrieval accomplished by one of our enemies.

The Vietnam War:

*A*nother important event happened when the Vietnam War ended with the fall of Saigon on the 30th of April, 1975. One thing barely mentioned for much of the conflict was our involvement in aiding the North Vietnamese as a proxy war against America. In the mid-1960s, we had North

Vietnamese pilots and anti-aircraft gunners being trained within our country to familiarize them with the weapons we were supplying, while some of our troops even manned anti-aircraft guns within North Vietnam to shoot down American pilots. Our aid also increased as the war progressed, to where we were supplying North Vietnam with the majority of their war supplies. This included various military weapons, armored vehicles, food, fuel, ammunition and other necessary items. It was an outcome when our country was covertly fighting against America through the use of military support. The same could be said in our Afghanistan campaign where America supplied the Mujahideen fighters with lethal weapons to use against us only a few years later. Many would eventually compare our Afghanistan War with America's Vietnam.

Third Phase Summary:

During the 1960s, the Soviet attack submarine force abandoned its pattern of local fleet area exercises for an ambitious program of distant area deployments. The evolution of this Soviet attack submarine force also reflected the changing naval threats. Soviet responses to new threats resulted in four general phases of submarine development. During this third phase from 1967 to 1975, the Soviet Union introduced the first in a series of attack submarines designed for anti-submarine warfare (ASW), which was a natural response to the large Polaris submarine force which the US was developing since the early 1960s. These new Soviet attack submarines combined nuclear propulsion with the latest systems to achieve higher underwater speeds, more sensitive sonar, and increased depth capabilities. These improvements were meant to detect, intercept and trail US submarines. This led to the final phase of Soviet submarine development, which was to modernize the Soviet submarine fleet using advanced construction methods, including stealth technologies, quieter operations, and more lethal weapons.

1976 to 1991 Phase
The Modernization Of Soviet Submarines:

Starting in the mid 1970s, the Soviet Union began a comprehensive modernization of their defense industry, which included the construction of modern manufacturing facilities, and the installation of state-of-the-art machinery and equipment. They also incorporated major capital improvements within other defense areas like submarine construction. New submarine designs and weapons systems required more extensive use of high-strength materials like titanium and composites, which required specialized machining capabilities. New materials, complex shapes, and the miniaturization needed in many advanced systems—such as for cruise missile guidance and submarine propulsion systems—demanded more sophisticated equipment. As legal imports of Western plant and equipment soared during the late 1970s, this enabled many Soviet defense plants to produce advanced weapons much earlier than was possible using older equipment.

This commitment to Soviet defense modernization was helped by the rise of Dmitriy Ustinov, who had been gaining power from the mid-1960s. He had long advocated for implementing Western style management techniques, and his appointment to the position of Minister of Defense in 1976, with the subsequent appointment of like-minded subordinates, coalesced Soviet views towards his defense-industrial modernization policies. Attesting to the progress the Soviets made in modernizing their defense industries was the number of new systems in production that demanded relatively advanced manufacturing equipment. While implemented within the general military, it also went within submarine systems and weapons to create advanced generations of submarines. (See Figure 44 for Modern submarine chronology.) In addition, earlier submarine designs such as the Delta class received important weapons improvements.

1976 Delta-III Class

The Delta-III class SSBN (*Project 667BDR Kalmar*) was another upgrade from the earlier Delta-I and Delta-II submarines, and carried fourteen of the latest SS-N-18 Stingray (*R-29R*) ballistic missiles. These submarine-launched ballistic missiles were the first ones to have multiple independently targeted reentry vehicles (MIRVs) which allowed each missile to hit multiple targets. (See Figure 45 on modern ballistic missile evolution.) The nuclear-powered Delta-III class started entering service in 1976, and had a submerged speed of 24 knots. They included an overall length of 508 feet. For additional armament, each unit had four 21-inch torpedo tubes at the bow, with room to carry up to sixteen ASW and anti-ship torpedoes. They had an operating depth limit of 1310 feet. Fourteen units entered service from 1976 to 1981, and each carried a crew of 130. Like the earlier Delta-I and Delta-II versions, these were meant to bypass the US SOSUS detection system by being able to launch ballistic missiles away from any detection areas. The Delta-III class submarines also had upgraded navigation and sonar abilities, including the ability to fire all onboard ballistic missiles in one single salvo. (See Figure 47 on page 130.)

Due to these newer Delta-III submarines carrying ballistic missiles containing MIRVs, starting in 1978 the Soviet Union began removing the ballistic missiles from fourteen of their Yankee-I class submarines.

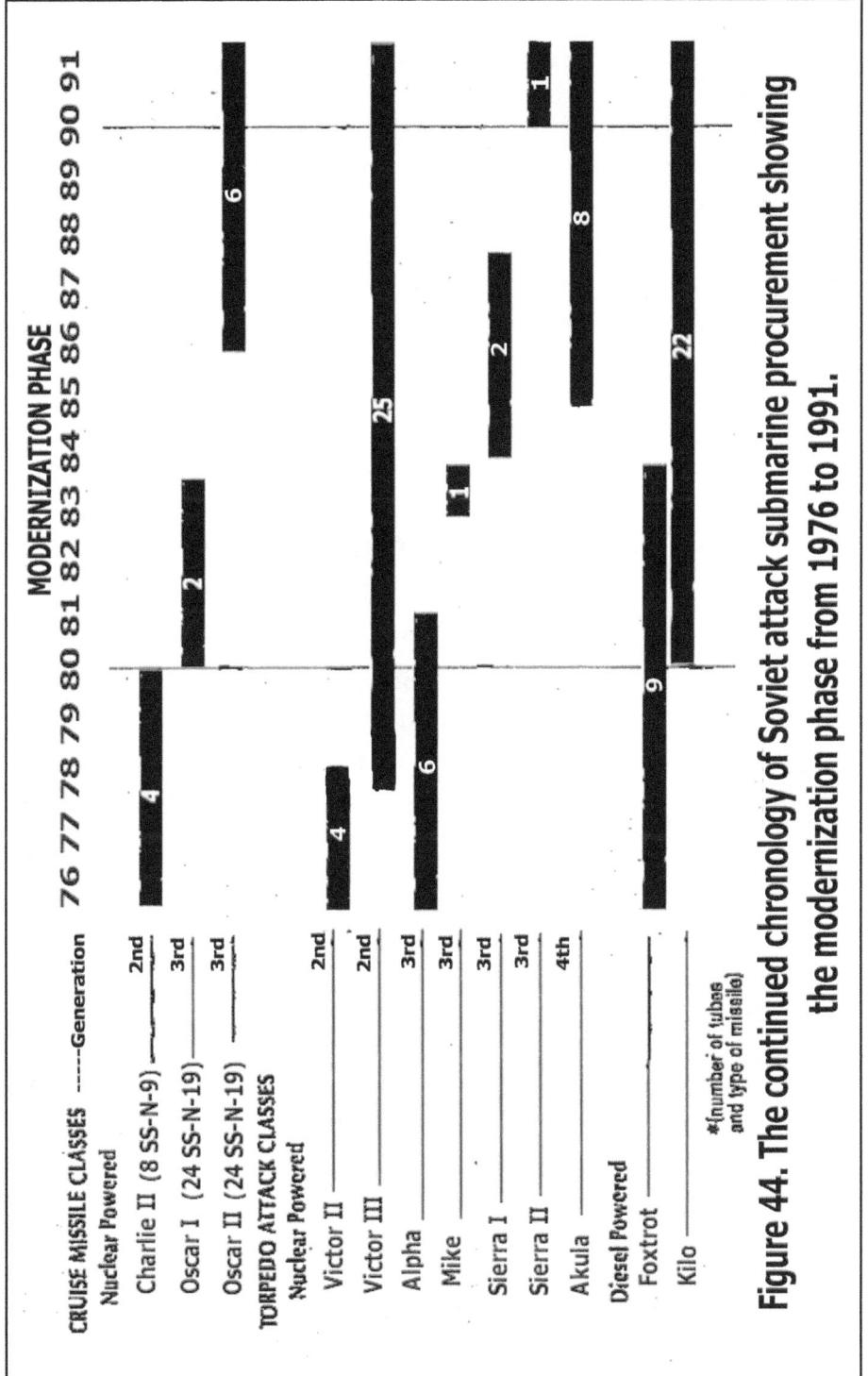

Figure 44. The continued chronology of Soviet attack submarine procurement showing the modernization phase from 1976 to 1991.

This was done to remain in compliance with the Salt I Interim Agreement signed in 1972 by President Nixon and Soviet leader Brezhnev, and was due to the agreement limitations of 62 nuclear-powered ballistic missile submarines, and 950 submarine-launched ballistic missiles per country. As a result, three of the Yankee-I units were converted into attack submarines having cruise missile capabilities, and these were called the Yankee Notch version. Another conversion was called the Yankee Sidecar where one submarine was converted to carry twelve SS-NX-24 cruise missiles. Other Yankee-I submarines were eventually converted into additional SSN torpedo attack units, or were changed into various experimental models.

Modern Soviet War Strategy:

The Soviets wrote that in wartime they would attempt to interdict Western sea lines of communication by conducting missile and air strikes against enemy ports, by sinking merchant and troop transport ships on the high seas, and by sowing mines in heavily traveled waters. Soviet emphasis on all three of these basic methods was a departure from the views of their past interdiction theory.

Soviet authors, for example, had stressed that a major flaw in German planning during World War Two was their failure to mount massive and systematic attacks on enemy shipping ports. The tone of the Soviet discussion about German mistakes suggested that on European ports, such attacks with conventional weapons would be launched if a war did not escalate into a nuclear conflict. Soviet theorists noted that once the nuclear threshold was crossed, nuclear strikes against land targets were the most efficient means to interdict shipping. Similarly, the Soviets also had stated in the past that mining operations were underestimated as a means of disrupting normal shipping routes.

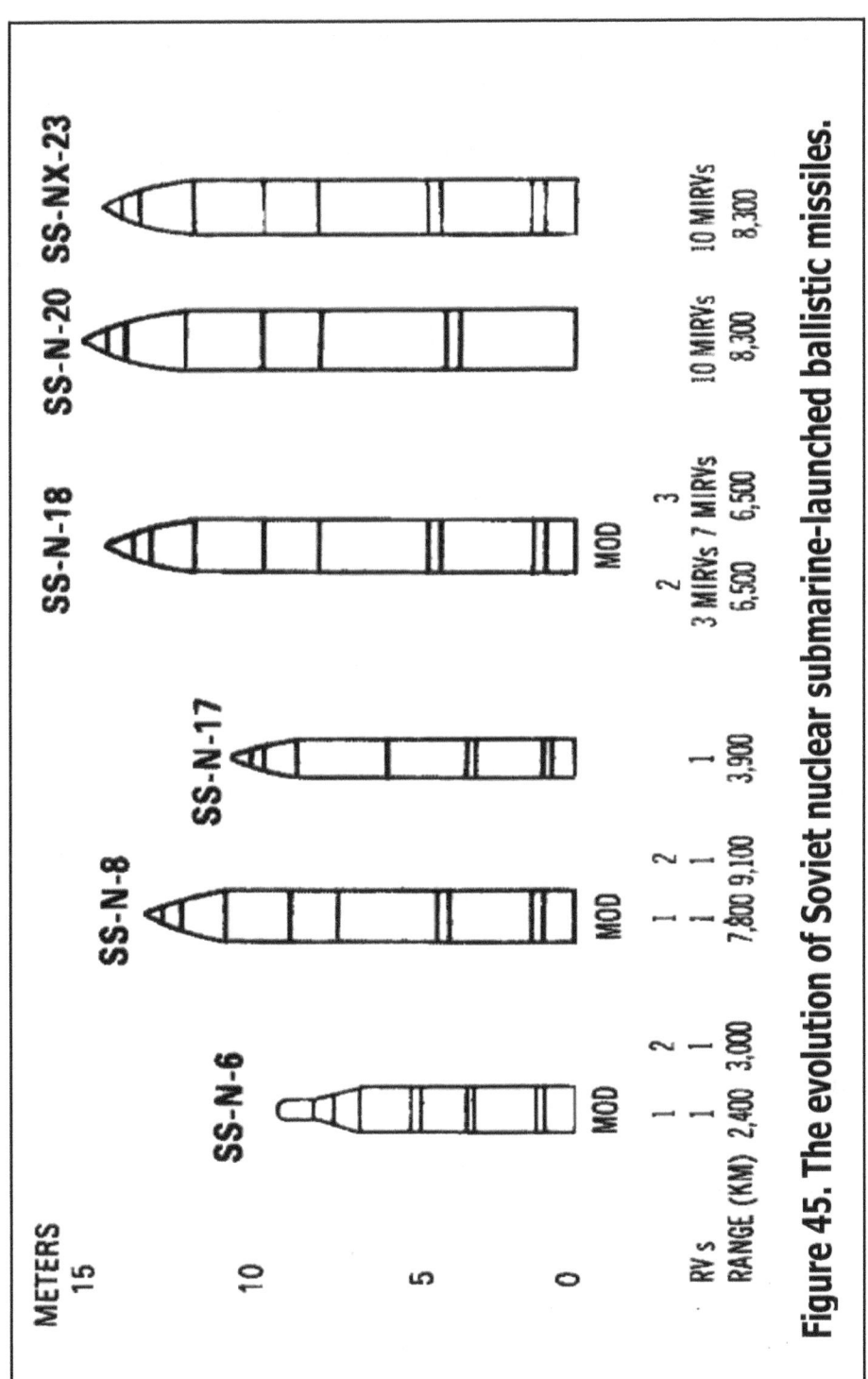

Figure 45. The evolution of Soviet nuclear submarine-launched ballistic missiles.

Mine warfare in their view was useful because it could strain enemy naval resources, and would extend the amount of time that merchant ships must remain at sea, thus enhancing their vulnerability to other forms of attack.

In 1978 the USSR had the ability to threaten the shipping lanes on which the United States was economically and militarily dependent. There were, however, various interpretations as to how many Soviets forces might be needed for such a mission. To this end, the Soviets also firmly believed that an effective means to interdict shipping was through attacking an enemy's ports and harbors. Thus, Soviet capabilities to conduct an at-sea interdiction campaign was a key element for an assessment of Soviet options in a variety of potential conflict scenarios. Regardless of how any conflict began, they would have included their general purpose naval forces toward the destruction of US aircraft carriers and ballistic missile submarines.

In open ocean interdiction, Soviet attack submarines would be the primary strike force. Aviation would have a dual role—to participate in anti-shipping strikes and to locate targets. Surface ships, in the Soviet view, would be needed to support and protect their submarines transiting to and from the sea lanes. The Soviets would have only deployed their surface ships within effective range of their land-based aircraft. This emphasis on coordinated operations, coupled with the use of air cover, might dictate concentrations of Soviet forces within a few hundred miles from Europe, with only a few Soviet submarines operating alone in distant waters. If sufficient forces were available, the Soviets might have tried to create a submarine threat within the entire naval theater because they also viewed interdiction as a useful diversionary tactic. They knew that it would be easier to attack than to defend merchant ships, and consequently, that a few submarines could tie up a disproportionate amount of an enemy's resources. For example, for each

German U-boat used during the Second World War, the Allies were obligated to deploy twenty-five ASW ships and one-hundred aircraft, something not to be lost with time.

The Soviets regarded the aircraft carrier as a key element to Western general purpose naval forces, as a reserve strategic nuclear force, and was an integral part for amphibious landing forces. Most of the Soviet Navy's cruise missile submarines and air-to-surface missile aircraft were designed primarily to counter Western aircraft carriers, although these forces could be employed against any ships at sea. As the US further deployed large numbers of submarine-launched ballistic missile units, the Soviets began to focus on the Polaris submarine as a primary strategic naval threat to the USSR. Assuming that the Soviets gave at-sea interdiction the same priority as that to anti-submarine and anti-carrier warfare, they could assign twenty-one long-range torpedo attack submarines—about thirty percent of the general purpose submarines in their Northern Fleet—to interdict North Atlantic shipping.

How much time Soviet submarines were to spend in the sea lanes per patrol might come from a general rule that the Soviets seemed to accept, and was gained from German experiences obtained during the Second World War. While operating new submarines from forward bases in France and Norway, the Germans were able to keep only a third of their forces on station at any one time. Therefore, from the USSR's more distant bases in the Northern Fleet, less time could be spent on station, assuming similar conditions. The estimates of submarine turnaround times for such a scenario were also based on other German experiences. The Germans averaged during World War Two more than three weeks between patrols. If the Soviets spent a like amount of time between patrols, their nuclear submarines could operate on the sea lanes about forty percent of the time, with their diesel submarines only at about thirty percent. In a long campaign, additional time would be required for extended maintenance—an area characterized by poor Soviet performance even during peacetime. By comparison, the Germans—while using newer and less sophisticated submarines—found it necessary to make extensive repairs after every seven or eight wartime patrols. In addition, the size of a likely US re-supply effort—while providing numerous targets for Soviet submarines—would work against a Soviet interdiction campaign. US plans for re-supplying NATO in a conventional war assumed a large scale of support shipping that would increase steadily during any protracted war.

Eventually, the pool of shipping committed to the re-supply of Europe would have increased substantially through additional allocations of Western European ships. However, the available Soviet submarine force clearly was inadequate to continuously deploy enough strike forces along the sea lanes. Therefore, when faced with a choice on how to solve this dilemma, the Soviets evidently would direct more forces against what they regarded as shipping's most vulnerable points—by attacking enemy ports with bombs and missiles, and by mining entrances to enemy harbors, with their Soviet submarine forces being used for any distant mining operations.

In 1979 the introduction of the latest Victor class unit further improved on their anti-carrier and mining capabilities, including a further reduction in the technology gap with opposing US attack submarines.

1979 Victor-III Class

The Victor-III class SSN (*Project 671RTM/RTMK Shchuka*) attack submarine was an improved version of the earlier Victor-II class which included a distinctive pod above the vertical tail that housed a towed sonar. This passive hydro-acoustic system allowed for the detection of enemy targets at greater ranges. (See Figure 46.)

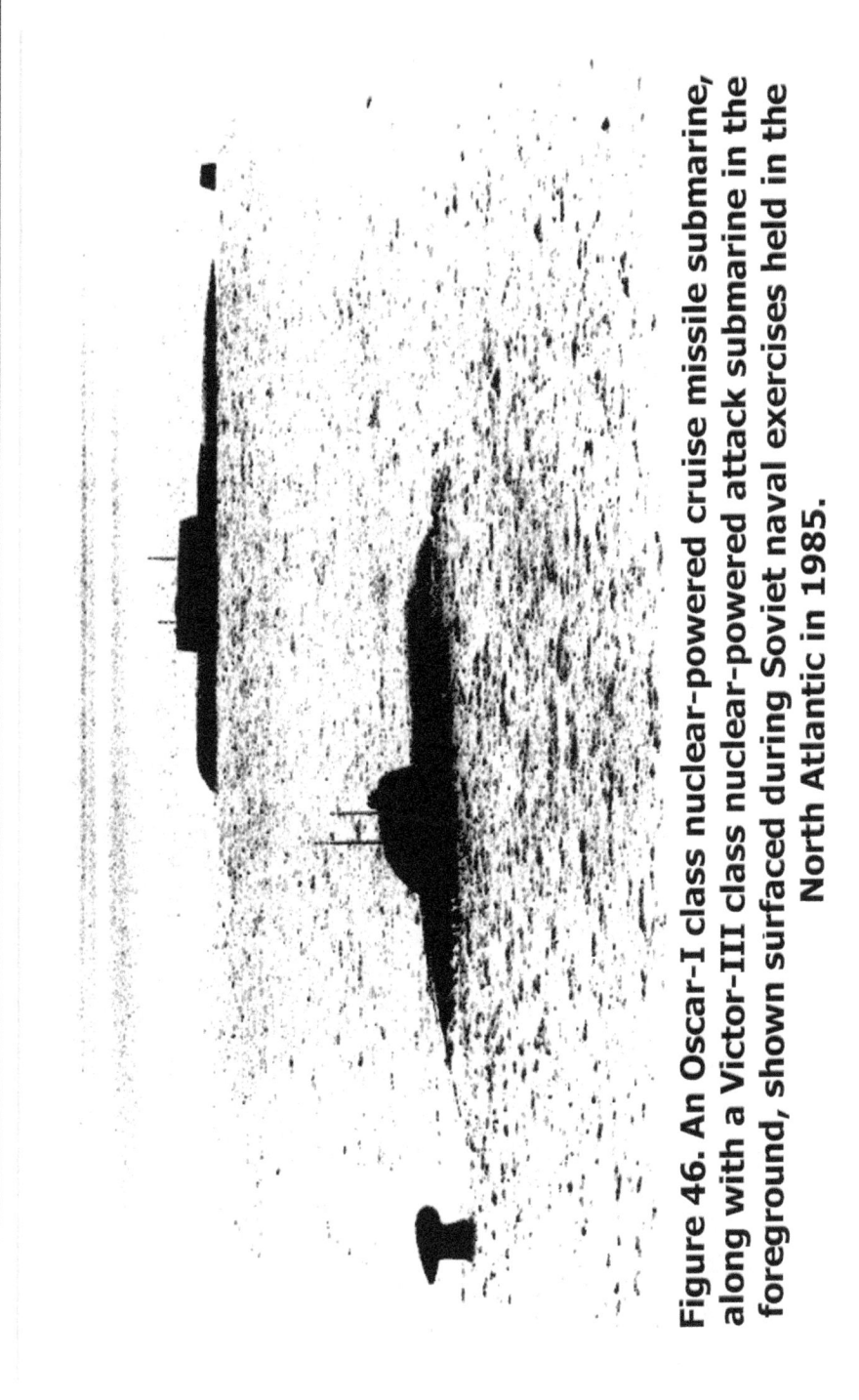

Figure 46. An Oscar-I class nuclear-powered cruise missile submarine, along with a Victor-III class nuclear-powered attack submarine in the foreground, shown surfaced during Soviet naval exercises held in the North Atlantic in 1985.

The Victor-III class also carried an improved version of the 65-73 super torpedoes. This newer 65-76 model included acoustic wake following for the targeting of enemy aircraft carriers, and could be launched from any depths. Other improvements occurred in navigation and communications systems, including with noise reduction. There were twenty-five Victor-III nuclear-powered submarines produced before the end of the Cold War, and each had an overall length of 348 feet. Their operating depth limit was 1310 feet. For armament each had four 21-inch torpedo tubes and two additional 25.6-inch torpedo tubes, all at the bow. They could carry up to six super torpedoes, along with eighteen regular torpedoes, or up to thirty-six naval mines. Each carried a crew of ninety-four.

Figure 47. The Delta-III class nuclear-powered ballistic missile submarine was the first to have multiple independently targeted reentry vehicles (MIRVs). These allowed for each missile to hit multiple targets.

Collision On The Surface:

There was another accident that was little known during our Soviet years, and it involved a submarine collision with a ship, and also a unique rescue. This all began at night on the 21st of October, 1980, when our Whiskey class submarine S-178 was returning to base while surfaced off of Skryplev Island near Vladivostok. The weather outside was very cold, with deteriorating conditions under total darkness. An outbound refrigeration ship named Refrizherator-13 was given permission to leave through the same inlet that they had just given our sub S-178 permission to enter. It was standard protocol for a surfaced submarine to have the right-of-way over a ship, but the sub's navigational lights were mistaken for a fishing boat by the ship, and the ship's navigational lights hadn't been turned on by the captain in charge for fear of being denied exit due to bad weather. And while the approaching ship in the inlet was picked up by the sonar-man aboard the submarine, this wasn't reported to the commander stationed up in the sail. As both vessels continued moving towards each other in poor visibility, it wasn't until they were too close that the ship was finally spotted, then the submarine's rudder was put over hard-to-starboard. In all the resulting confusion it was too late. The ship struck the submarine on her port side, opening a hole in her hull approximately two feet in diameter back by the sixth compartment. At 1945 local time the submarine quickly sank to the bottom of the inlet and settled down at a depth of thirty-two meters, with a thirty degree starboard list.

It must be pointed out that there were many lax decisions made by both vessels leading up to this accident. The lack of running lights by the ship, the misidentification of the submarine, the local authorities allowing both vessels to enter the inlet at the same time, the submarine not closing compartments and not being at quarters. Too many aboard the submarine were already mentally at the dock instead of being concerned with safely navigating the inlet. By this time the Refrizherator-13 had radioed to shore about the accident and emergency buoys were released from the submarine at the bottom. Already five seamen aboard the submarine had drowned. The sub's commander along with ten others were thrown off the bridge in the collision, and seven of them were picked up by the colliding ship.

Inside the submarine, the surviving crew had fled from the flooded central compartments, and moved forward and aft. Here they assessed the situation, while waiting for a rescue vessel to arrive at the scene. This took approximately two hours. Meanwhile, a careless seaman lit some fuel floating in the bilges on fire in the second compartment while smoking, which was extinguished using the VPL air-foam system. Moments later it flared up again and had to be put out a second time. Then radio communications was finally established with the rescue vessel above them. They were told a rescue submarine would be arriving within a day, and would station underwater next to them. A rescue plan was devised that would use divers to pass a messenger line from one sub to the other. This was in the hope that they could escape through the torpedo tubes and swim over to the awaiting sub through the freezing water.

During the next day they successfully placed the line after the rescue submarine had arrived on station. Then a short while later two seamen in the forward compartment attempted to escape—but after leaving the torpedo tube—they couldn't find the line and were forced to swim all the way up to the surface using emergency breathing equipment. Six others made an attempt later that evening and were successfully met by divers, who helped transfer them over to the rescue submarine. Another seaman passed out after exiting the torpedo tube and ended up floating to the surface on his own. More attempts continued. Six more ended up dying. Also attempting an escape were the four seamen who were trapped back in the seventh compartment, they all ended up leaving through a stern torpedo tube. However, without finding the messenger line, they were forced to swim up to the surface as well. So the end result was only twenty-one made it out alive and survived the collision, while thirty-one ended up dying. Some that had left by torpedo tubes were never found. The submarine was later raised by using pontoons and towed to shallow water, then was placed into drydock. An inspection was made with a determination that the submarine was beyond repair, and so she was stricken. A trial was later held that accused both the ship's captain and the sub's commander of negligence. The court found them both guilty and sentenced each of them to ten years of imprisonment.

Operation Ivy Bells:

During the Cold War, our country used an undersea communications cable that linked our Pacific Fleet naval base at Petropavlovsk to our mainland Pacific Fleet headquarters situated in Vladivostok. This connecting cable went through the Sea of Okhotsk and was protected by various listening devices, including normal sea-based patrols to detect any intruders. It was also situated within our own territorial waters. However, a curious situation developed in 1980 when a retired American NSA worker named Roger Pelton entered our Soviet embassy in Washington, D.C., and sold us information about the eavesdropping that was being done on this cable by American military intelligence. It went by the code name of Operation Ivy Bells, and was made possible through the use of a covert US Navy submarine, the USS Halibut, that was capable of entering our waters undetected and placing a recording device that tapped into this cable to intercept our fleet communications. Once a month this device was retrieved by divers from this American submarine, and a *new device replaced it to continue recording more data. This program was expanded to other cables we had in our undersea communications network, until we discovered through this insider the existence of this secret spy operation, and eventually removed all the recorders.*

1980 Submarine Torpedoes:

Soviet torpedo evolution saw another improvement in 1980 when the dual purpose USET-80 heavyweight torpedo entered service, and was to become one of the main torpedoes carried aboard Soviet submarines. The USET-80 was a 21-inch diameter torpedo using passive acoustic homing against enemy submarines that switched to active acoustic homing during the terminal phase. Against ships and carriers, it used acoustic wake following.

Further refinements with its sensors happened in later years for improved running in shallow waters and under ice, along with updated batteries for faster propulsion. Also at the same time a new Kilo class submarine entered service, along with the prototype Yankee-II class and the Oscar class. The Soviet Navy then would see the arrival of the largest submarine ever built for service, the Typhoon class.

1980 Kilo Class

The Kilo class SS (*Project 877 Paltus*) was a new generation of Soviet diesel-electric submarines meant for ASW operations in shallower waters, and also for general patrolling and mine laying. They started entering service in 1980, and had a submerged speed of seventeen knots. (See Figure 48.) They included an overall length of only 229 feet and had six 21-inch torpedo tubes at the bow, with room to carry up to eighteen ASW torpedoes or twenty-four mines.

Figure 48. The Kilo class diesel-powered attack submarine was designed for conducting anti-submarine operations in shallower waters.

Figure 49. The Sierra class nuclear-powered attack submarine, with a towed-array sonar pod, first became operational in 1984.

Each Kilo class submarine had an operating depth limit of 1150 feet. A total of twenty-two units went into service for the Soviet Union, and each carried a crew of fifty-seven.

This submarine had a pressurized double-hull and was considered very quiet for a diesel electric. In later years there were significant upgrades made to the Kilo class that improved further on their stealth abilities.

1980 Yankee-II Class

The Yankee-II class SSBN (*Project 667AM Navaga-M*) was a 2nd generation submarine converted from an earlier Yankee-I class to carry twelve SS-N-17 Snipe (*R-31*) ballistic missiles. Only one submarine conversion was completed as a prototype in 1980, and this was the only Soviet submarine ever fitted with these ballistic missiles. The SS-N-17 Snipe was the first solid-fuel missile deployed on a submarine, but had only half the range of the SS-N-8 version, so further development was therefore discontinued. This single unit remained in service for only about ten years before being dismantled at Severodvinsk.

1980 Oscar-I Class

The Oscar-I class SSGN (*Project 949 Granit*) was a 3rd generation nuclear-powered cruise missile submarine which improved on the earlier Charlie-II class by carrying twenty-four long-range anti-ship SS-N-19 cruise missiles. These submarines were meant to confront carrier groups by firing all of their missiles in such quantity that they would overwhelm an enemy's defenses. This version also improved on the earlier Charlie-II class by having a dual nuclear reactor with two propeller shafts, which increased their top speed. They were to become the largest cruise missile submarines ever built by the Soviet Union. (See Figure 50.)

The first of only two Oscar-I units became operational starting in 1980, and they had an overall length of 508 feet. For additional armament there were two 25.6-inch torpedo tubes, along with four 21-inch torpedo tubes, all at the bow. Each unit had room to carry up to four super torpedoes and four regular torpedoes, and were capable of firing both the SS-N-15 Starfish and the SS-N-16 anti-submarine weapons.

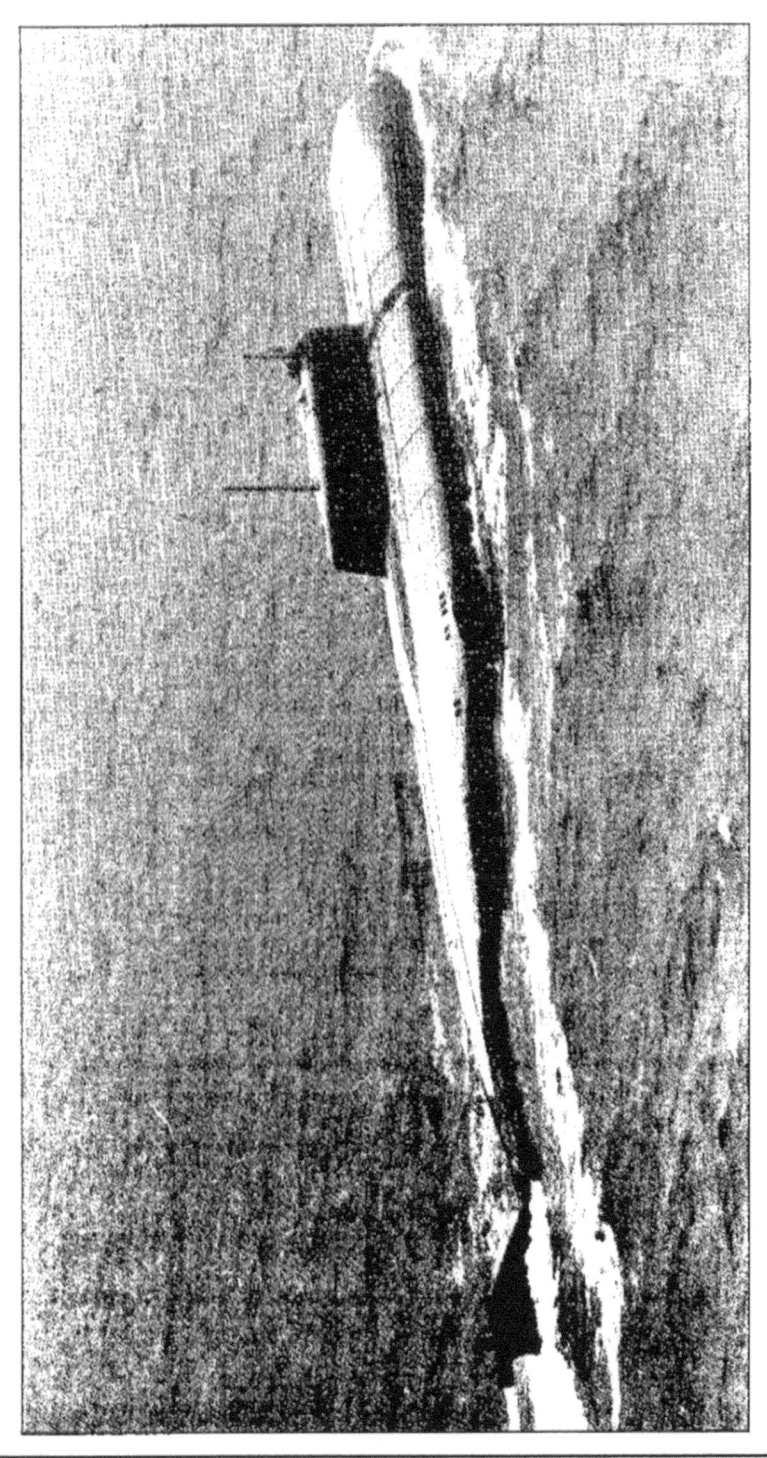

Figure 50. The Oscar class was the largest nuclear-powered cruise missile submarine built by the Soviet Union. Two versions were built based on different total lengths.

They had an operating depth limit of 1640 feet, and each carried a crew of ninety-four. This submarine improved on the Charlie-II class by having a top speed of thirty-two knots while being submerged. However, an updated Oscar class was needed with additional room for improving the layout of its weapon and machinery spaces, including the ability to carry more torpedoes. The Oscar-II class (*Project 949A Antey*) entered service in 1986, and six units were completed for the Soviet Union.

1982 Typhoon Class

The Soviet Typhoon class SSBN (*Project 941 Akula*) was the Soviet's first entirely new SSBN design since the Yankee-I class was introduced in 1966. It was significantly quieter than earlier SSBNs and incorporated ice-penetrating features into its design to facilitate surface launches from the Arctic icepack. Typhoon submarines routinely conducted under-ice operations. (See Figure 51.) Three Typhoons were originally built, then others were added as older Echo-Is and Echo-IIs were retired.

They started entering service in 1982, and carried twenty SS-N-20 Sturgeon (*R-39*) ballistic missiles that had up to ten MIRVs each. They also had six 21-inch torpedo tubes at the bow, and could carry up to twenty-two USET-80 torpedoes. They had a submerged speed of 27 knots, and had an operating depth limit of 3000 feet due to their special titanium hull. These were the largest submarines ever built with an overall length of 574 feet. However, their massive size also turned out to be a curse, as it was difficult to break through the ice and have all the missile silos cleared for launching. They were designed with a complicated number of pressure hulls that effectively created two separate submarines within a single outer hull. They also had escape capsules and used special ice-breaking features.

Figure 51. The Typhoon class was the largest nuclear-powered ballistic missile submarine built by the Soviet Union. Capable of staying submerged for months at a time, each unit had a top speed of 27 knots and carried a crew of 168.

The Soviets included an extremely low frequency ELF communications system that enabled them to contact other SSBNs while under normal operating conditions. Each Typhoon class submarine carried a crew of 168, and only six units were completed before the Cold War ended.

A Standoff In Sweden:

On the morning of October 28, 1981, an oil slick mysteriously appeared along an island in southern Sweden, and this was seen by a couple of local Swedish fishermen returning from a morning trip out of the inlet. Upon investigating the source of the spill, one of them noticed something stranded on the shallow rocks nearby. It turned out it was our Whiskey class submarine S-363 that had run aground, and there was an armed seaman standing guard on deck to keep any outsiders from climbing aboard. One of the fishermen notified the closest Swedish naval base about this, and what followed was a chain of events that nearly brought both of our countries into a state of war.

At first things remained calm after the discovery until about an hour later when a Swedish patrol boat reached our stricken submarine, and demanded answers. They seemed unsatisfied after being told that the inadvertent stranding happened due to a navigational error while running submerged. It must be emphasized that Sweden had learned not to trust our navy, as they had fired on us before when we inadvertently went inside their territorial waters by accident. We knew that they were secretly helping the West by spying on our activities in the Baltic, so the feelings were often mutual. And as time passed, more Swedish boats came out to the area to observe our submarine and try to demand answers from the captain. Meanwhile, our own fleet was contacted for assistance, as Moscow gave an explanation that wasn't believed by

Swedish officials. But we did muster up some ships to give a show of force, including a missile destroyer, should anything happen while our tugs attempted to pull our submarine back off the rocks. Also an order was issued to blow up the submarine should any attempts be made to confiscate her. But before this escalated any further, negotiations were held that eventually lasted ten days, including allowing an interrogation of our sub's captain. Then a final solution was made by Swedish authorities to not allow Soviet tugs to assist, instead they used their own tugs to pull our submarine back into the strait, and off she went. So a war was averted, and this incident forever became known by the West as "Whiskey on the rocks".

Hurried Out To Sea:

Another unfortunate accident happened in June of 1983, when one of our submarines was needed to take part in military exercises being conducted off the shores of Kamchatka. K-429 was the Charlie class submarine chosen for this task, but had recently returned to base from an earlier patrol. This meant that the entire crew was already away on leave while repairs and re-supply were happening to the submarine. However, the departed captain was notified and told to prepare his crew to return to base immediately, and without delay. So many were successfully recalled, but some couldn't be located. The captain told the Soviet commander at Pacific Fleet headquarters that it wouldn't be safe to proceed on such a mission when so many were still absent, yet he was told not to question his decision—just get out to sea as ordered! So to round out the missing crew, the captain filled a third of them using sailors from other nearby submarines stationed at the base. Hastily this all occurred, and the sub was readied as ordered. None of the new crewmembers received any special training prior to departure.

On June 23rd in the evening they cleared the dock, and headed out to the testing area for a first dive. At this point, the watch still hadn't been properly set, yet the order was given to take the submarine down to periscope depth. How it happened few would believe, but the submarine wasn't prepared to dive since the instruments hadn't been properly set—nor was all the required crew at their assigned control stations. More importantly, the valves that needed to be closed prior to diving were all still open, and as the operator had the submarine diving as ordered, flooding immediately started in the forward compartments. The captain tried to counter this by blowing ballast, but the inexperienced console operator incorrectly blew the tanks out the top without releasing any ballast. One seaman opened a forward hatch and reported the massive flooding to the warrant officer in the adjacent compartment, then went back into the flooding compartment and closed the hatch behind him. This is where his drowned body was eventually found. He had obeyed the rule of the fleet—to never abandon a stricken compartment on his own. Then the crew felt the bow of the submarine strike the bottom of Sarannaya Bay, and settle down at a depth of thirty-eight meters.

At this point the captain ascertained that compartments one, two, four and five were still flooding, so these were evacuated of the remaining sailors. Already fourteen of them had died due to drowning. Another problem that confronted the crew was the emergency buoys had been welded to the hull to prevent them from being lost at sea. This meant no distress signal and they would have to attempt to reach the surface using the escape hatch. Next the nuclear reactor was shut down to prevent any accident, and this was accomplished without incident. After some time and deciding that help was not arriving, the captain asked for two volunteers the next morning to attempt an escape. None of the crew had any experience using the escape hatch before, so this was a particularly dangerous task for any of them, but two agreed to try an escape to alert others above. They put on the standard scuba-gear and were given a note with an explanation of the situation aboard their submarine for the rescuers, then one of them attempted to leave through the escape hatch.

Meanwhile, back on the surface there had been an alert issued for the missing submarine after they had not surfaced from the first test dive and reported back that all was well. A ship had been dispatched and was looking along the route the submarine had taken out to the training area, however nothing was seen on the surface. But then they did find something–it was the floating dead body of the first seaman that had volunteered to leave the submarine. Inside the sunken submarine, the captain had decided to send out only one person and then wait for a rescue, since he assumed the first diver had made it safely to the surface. Meanwhile, gasses from cracked batteries were starting to make breathing difficult inside for the crew. Then things got worse overnight, and still no sign of any rescue. The following morning they could wait no longer, since battery wells began exploding one by one. It was time to get out! At 1100 the crew started to leave through the escape hatch, and upon reaching the surface, they were picked up by awaiting vessels conducting searches above.

Afterwards, some divers from a rescue ship were sent down with supplies for the remaining trapped sailors. This was placed in the escape hatch and was welcomed since their oxygen canister supplies had been depleted. This allowed the rest of the crew to escape from the submarine later that day, although two more died in the process. It had taken nearly twelve hours for everyone to finally escape! A later head count showed that of the total crew that originally left, in total eighteen lives were lost in her sinking. The submarine was later successfully floated and towed to nearby Sovetsky. A trial was held for the captain after being charged with negligence for the handling of his submarine. He was convicted and sentenced to ten years in prison.

Soviet Navy Living Conditions:

For many sailors, life in the Soviet Navy was considered harsh since they often put in many long hours with little time off. The Northern and Pacific fleets—being the largest and most important ones—had their base facilities located in desolate areas with bleak and cold climates. The resulting morale difficulties were made worse by an unwillingness on the part of the Soviet leadership to devote sufficient resources to alleviate these difficult living conditions. Career personnel often fared better than the conscripts, although they too suffered from the effects of assignments in remote areas, particularly on their family lives. Recreational facilities at most naval bases were practically nonexistent, so sailors depended on trips to the nearest towns for relief from boredom. Political officers, in their attempts to arrange for entertainment on base, were hampered by the lack of available resources, and also confused entertainment with indoctrination. A Soviet admiral noted how the following movie titles were being shown to his various outfits—*The Communist Party as the Organizer and Inspirer of the Great October Socialist Revolution. Lenin, the Founder of the Soviet State. The Friendship of the Peoples of the Socialist Community. We Are Building Communism.* Most sailors probably felt little recreation when watching any of these movies.

Another problem with naval moral was that conscripts were paid very little. A naval infantryman who served in the Black Sea Fleet said parents had to mail him money just so he could afford to eat a decent meal in the servicemen's club. Leave and liberty were rarely granted for most conscripts.

The general Soviet approach seemed to be to keep them confined to the base where their activities could be more easily monitored and controlled. Most conscripts received one ten-day leave period during their term of service. Liberty policies varied greatly from unit to unit. One unit was allowed only one five-hour liberty every three months, although a more commonly reported figure was one six-hour pass on weekends. Career sailors received thirty days of leave a year (forty-five if they served on nuclear submarines) and had evenings free while in home port.

The sea experiences that Soviet naval officers received was strikingly different from that of their US counterparts. In general, the United States operated a steaming navy with a high operational tempo. The Soviet Navy outside of the submarine fleet, by contrast, conserved their equipment during peacetime and emphasized readiness to go to sea, so that most of the time Soviet officers spent aboard their ships occurred in port, at anchorages, or on short cruises of a day or two. US carrier deployments in the Pacific averaged about eight months, with over five and a half months spent underway. A Soviet Pacific Fleet deployment typically ran for only one to five months, with most of the time spent in ports or anchorages. On average, only about ten percent of the Soviet surface fleet was deployed away from Soviet home waters at any one time. Military exercises in the Soviet Navy were often characterized by short and carefully planned drills, with little or no free play among participants.

An example of the lack of realism in Soviet sea training was provided by a 1982 Red Star article written by a submariner and a surface ASW officer. They both described an ASW exercise that followed cut-and-dried patterns. The ASW ship commander reduced his risks to the minimum by repeatedly waiting for the target submarine to move from one assigned point to the next. The submarine commander didn't try to shake off his pursuer because only the surface ship commander was being evaluated for the exercise.

Moreover, the actions of the submarine were all planned in advance by the ASW staff to ensure that a contact could be easily made by the surface ship.

Another issue encountered was that only a small number of women were in the Soviet Navy, and that they almost always served in the enlisted ranks, holding jobs such as radio or telephone operator, typist, nurse, supply clerk, or cook. There were no women ever placed into combat roles, and Naval careers didn't appear to be popular among Soviet women. Many female sailors were married to career Navy men, and many only enlisted because civilian jobs were oftentimes hard to come by around remote garrisons. During conversations with naval personnel, Soviet officers generally disparaged the practice of allowing women to serve in the Navy. Even in later years the Soviets made few improvements to their practices. If greater career opportunities were available to them, the Soviet Navy might have attracted more educated women who could have helped to ease the problems resulting from demographic changes within their country. Even if they weren't employed in combat billets, more women used in more responsible roles could have freed up others and improved their ranks in the process.

Soviet Leadership Changes:

Important changes in Soviet leadership began after Leonid Brezhnev's health rapidly deteriorated in early 1982, and he died in office later that year. The eighteen-year term he served was second in duration only to that of Joseph Stalin. Yuri Andropov was chosen to replace him, and he became the sixth leader of the Soviet Union. Andropov served in the post from November of 1982 until his death in February of 1984. Andropov was succeeded by Konstantin Chernenko, who continued the same policies established during Andropov's tenure. However Chernenko served in office for even less time—only thirteen months. Like Andropov, Chernenko spent much of his time in a hospital, and he died while in office. In March of 1985 Chernenko was succeeded by Mikhail Gorbachev, who implemented perestroika and glasnost policies to reform the Soviet Union both politically and economically.

In the last years of the Brezhnev era, the Soviets had mapped out a strategy for speeding up the modernization of both their civilian and defense industries. This new focus was for a high-technology revolution, and a revitalization of their entire industrial base. Andropov continued that process by rejuvenating the bureaucracy with new managers which were better educated and more familiar with new technologies. The leadership under Gorbachev moved to reinforce the place of this science and technology policy as being the linchpin to their modern economic strategy. The military industry continued to be a vital piece in modernization, including the submarine fleet and weapons systems. During this time, two of the latest third generation submarines entered service, the Mike and Sierra classes, along with the final Delta class, the Delta-IV.

1983 Mike Class

The Mike class SSN (*Project 685 Plavnik*) was a nuclear-powered attack submarine that was capable of firing a wide range of submarine-launched weapons, including the SS-N-15 Starfish nuclear depth bomb, and both the SS-N-16 conventional and nuclear anti-submarine weapons. Only one submarine was ever built in this class, and it was considered to be an experimental model, however it also found use in protecting Soviet SSBNs. Its submerged speed was 30 knots, while it had a length of 385 feet. Due to its titanium inner hull, it quickly recorded a test dive down to an incredible depth of 3,350 feet. It also had an escape capsule built into the sail. For armament it had six 21-inch torpedo tubes with a quick loader at the bow, with room to carry up to twenty-two torpedoes or missile combinations. It had an operating depth limit of 4,100 feet and required a crew of sixty-nine. The only submarine of this class K-278 sank on April 7th, 1989.

1984 Delta-IV Class

The Delta-IV class SSBN (*Project 667BDRM Dolphin*) first entered service in 1984, and carried an improved ballistic missile–the SS-NX-23 Skiff (*R-29RM*). This missile was a liquid propelled ballistic missile that had a greater throw-weight, could carry up to ten MIRV warheads, and was more accurate than the SS-N-18 carried on the earlier Delta-IIIs. The Delta-IV submarine was twelve feet longer than the Delta-III, and had more efficient quieting designs such as a five bladed propeller, special hull coatings, and isolated machinery. The important potential of the Delta class was seen in the summer of 1981, when earlier Delta class submarines began conducting regular patrols in the marginal polar ice zone for surfacing through the ice to launch SS-N-8 SLBMs. The Delta class series–with the Delta-IV being the final modification–was mainly an extension of Yankee class SSBN technology. The SS-NX-23 was longer ranged and more accurate than its predecessor. The Delta-IV had an overall length of 547 feet, and an operating depth limit of 1310 feet. Each unit had four 21-inch torpedo tubes at the bow, and carried up to eighteen ASW torpedoes or SS-N-15 anti-ship weapons. Seven Delta-IV submarines entered service from 1984 to 1990, and each carried a crew of 135.

1984 Sierra-I Class

The Sierra-I class SSN (*Project 945 Barrakuda*) was a 3rd generation nuclear-powered attack submarine that was about twenty percent larger than the Victor-III class introduced only four years earlier. The Sierra-I class used advancements in submarine silencing such as applying special coatings to the hull, and included a built-in escape pod for emergencies. (See Figure 49 on page 135.) They could dive deeper than most earlier submarines due to a titanium hull–down to 1,800 feet. They started entering service in 1984, and were meant for engaging surface carrier fleets and for patrols in coastal regions. They had a submerged speed of 34 knots, and an overall length of 351 feet. Each unit had two 25.6-inch torpedo tubes at the bow, along with four 21-inch torpedo tubes, and could carry up to eight of the 65-76 super torpedoes, along with twenty regular torpedoes. As with the Mike class, it was capable of firing the SS-N-15 Starfish nuclear depth bomb, and both the SS-N-16 conventional and nuclear anti-submarine weapons. A total of three units went into service before the Cold War ended. A second version–the Sierra-II class (*Project 945A Kondor*) entered service in 1990. It was 16 feet longer and had two escape pods built into the sail. It also had improved sonar capabilities.

A Defector Defects

In August of 1985 one of our KGB agents went to the American embassy in Rome and told those inside he wanted to defect. He also promised to supply them with valuable information concerning two foreign spies we had working for us. This was greeted with great applause after it was made public in America, and was considered a major embarrassment for us since it would compromise a couple of our agents. Then a sudden turn of events happened. While being allowed to have dinner unattended a few blocks away from our Soviet embassy in Washington, D.C., our KGB agent casually walked out of that restaurant and slipped back into our Soviet embassy, then denied ever wanting to defect. Instead he accused the US government of kidnapping him in Rome, and then interrogating him at various secret locations—while promising him copious amounts of money for any secret information he had. This revelation was occurring a few weeks prior to a scheduled meeting between President Reagan and Soviet President Gorbachev, and was all explained at a press conference being hosted by Soviet officials. What was our embarrassment earlier had turned into an embarrassment for America. So was this all planned by us? Was he actually a double-agent acting on official orders? Who can say, but later he was greeted as a Soviet hero once he landed safely back home.

Soviet Navy Compensation:

Within the Soviet fleet, an officer's pay was based on rank, position, and length of service, with position pay constituting the largest share to an officer's income, being roughly double the pay received for rank, and it was awarded irrespective of rank. Thus, a commanding officer received more pay than an officer of equal rank in a non-command billet. Pay allowances and other benefits were also used to reward officers serving in assignments that were important to the Soviet fleet, but which involved family hardship or were dangerous or otherwise undesirable. Time served in the submarine fleet counted as double time for pension computation. Special bonuses were given for remote area assignments, with the biggest bonuses going to submariners on nuclear boats, under ice transfers, and equator crossings. Coveted assignments, higher promotional prospects, and other career inducements were also used as an incentive to attract the best officers to any critical areas. The importance of the submarine fleet, for example, was reflected in the dominance of submariners in a variety of key appointments.

Submariners were also promoted one year ahead of other officers at each rank level up to the level of Captain 1st.

All Soviet naval vessels, except for submarines, were officially dry. In recognition of their elite status and demanding duties, submariners were allowed one glass of wine or shot of vodka per day while at sea. Alcohol abuse wasn't a problem among submarine crews because of both strict discipline and a sense of pride and elitism. However, within the Soviet Navy surface fleet, they carried alcohol aboard for routine equipment maintenance, yet little of it was used for that purpose. Sailors in some units regularly took fifteen to twenty times the amounts authorized for their cleaning equipment and consumed it instead, while using only water or gasoline as a replacement. On one ship there was even a system for distributing the cleaning alcohol based on rank. Other cleaning products with alcohol bases were filtered through gas masks, ruining both the masks and the sailors who drank it. Parents could even contribute to this problem by mailing vodka to their sons serving in the Navy. Soviet press articles even criticized this practice, but some parents considered it their duty to try and ease the discomforts of service for them.

Many instances of theft and corruption often went unnoticed within the Soviet Navy according to Soviet press sources. A typical example of this appeared in a 1983 Red Star article, and was the case of a submarine commander who used his crew to work in a civilian industry. He was caught when a political officer noticed three new cars he had purchased in the last two years, which prompted an official investigation. Other instances had officers allowing their men to be used by civilian factories, and then ordering them to steal construction materials, vehicle parts, and food supplies for their units. Sailors were also caught selling state property, and in particular vehicle parts and clothing, on the outside black market to raise money to buy vodka. The Soviet Navy's personnel system indirectly encouraged commanders to cover up disciplinary infractions and unit performance problems such as these, since reporting such problems indicated how things weren't going well to naval authorities. The Soviet fleet seemed plagued by the same types of problems that Soviet society was having in general–including alcoholism, corruption, poor work habits, and absenteeism. Using military discipline and regimentation on recruits controlled these problems somewhat, but naval authorities still had trouble keeping them from affecting readiness. Heavy drinking was a part of the Russian culture for many centuries. Soviet studies linked alcohol use to eighty percent of the crimes committed in their country. It was also linked to many of the Navy's disciplinary problems as well.

A Secret Accident:

Many years and many submarine missions passed, and with so many it was not likely the true number of accidents could ever be recorded. Also, due to the nature of the Cold War, some things remained in secret for a reason, beyond what might seem obvious to those outside of the fleet. One such incident happened in the 1980s when a Soviet submarine in distress radioed out that they needed assistance due to an accident. Quickly, a dispatch was sent and a brief phone call was made. Little information could be given over the phone because of security concerns. The captain receiving the call was told to report immediately to a cruiser and to get underway as soon as possible–a nearby submarine was having a casualty. After hastily getting out of bed, he had just gotten dressed when a car showed up to take him to the nearby Soviet naval base. The ship was already notified and on alert, so after a fast car ride and boarding, the order was given to depart for sea. Upon clearing the lines and making way, the ship left on a course to rendezvous with the submarine that was surfaced and inbound. Then the order was given to anchor a ways out and wait for further orders, apparently this submarine was carrying nuclear warheads aboard and one of them was considered unstable for some unknown reason.

When the ship arrived at the area to anchor, the submarine was already present at a distance of about five nautical miles, so orders were changed to follow behind the submarine and report any actions. A few moments later the unthinkable happened. A cloud of smoke was spotted from the submarine, and one of her nuclear warheads was ejected into the air, and then made a splash into the ocean! The captain of the cruiser was still in shock over this, but after a moment of panic made the correct decision to have his navigator calculate the exact location of the nuclear warhead, and mark it on the chart. They then sailed to the spot of the splash and dropped a marker buoy over the sunken warhead. Days later after the stricken submarine was returned to base, the warhead was safely recovered and the involved personnel were instructed to never discuss this incident with anyone. Such were the ways of the Cold War.

Soviet Navy Discipline:

Despite the frugal living conditions found in much of the Soviet Navy, desertion wasn't considered a serious problem within the overall fleet. There were several likely reasons for that, including strict controls on personal travel and relocation within the Soviet Union. These travel restrictions made it easy for authorities to track down any deserters attempting to disappear and go back home. Punishment for those caught was severe, and usually involved a sentence to a disciplinary battalion. Moreover, at many bases in remote areas–there was simply nowhere for a deserter to go. A more common problem in home ports was unauthorized or over-extended liberty. Boredom seemed a strong incentive for going AWOL (absent without leave). It was an offense that typically carried a much lighter punishment, such as being given extra duties. However, in some units officers made little effort to stop sailors from sneaking off base at night, and throughout the Soviet Navy, warrant officers could be bribed for a pass. But in foreign ports discipline was more strict, and sailors weren't allowed ashore without being accompanied by an official escort.

The Soviet naval leadership placed little trust in their common sailors, and naval practices discouraged sailors from engaging in any activities that weren't closely monitored and controlled. In the Soviet fleet, senior conscripts ruled over junior ones. By tradition, new draftees were forced, often under the threat of physical violence, to serve on cleanup details, to do laundry, shine shoes, or perform other menial tasks. This informal hierarchy was tolerated, and even encouraged, by officers and warrant officers because it lightened up their supervisory duties.

Senior sailors were sometimes punished for being too easy on first-year conscripts. Commanders had considerable leeway in disciplining subordinates. Administrative discipline generally dealt with violations of military regulations such as communications security, dereliction of duty, and being absent without leave. Punishment options included an assignment of extra duties, denial for leave or liberty, demotions, or even brig sentences. A commanding officer sometimes delegated minor discipline matters to a military court composed of a sailor's peers.

Soviet sailors greatly feared being sent to the brig. Most naval brigs were overcrowded, and commanders often had to bribe wardens to get anyone admitted. Upon arrival, a sailor first had to have his head shaved, which was one of the worst consequences to a brig term because it was an embarrassing stigma after being released back to a unit. They also had all their non-issued clothing permanently confiscated, along with belts and hatbands that could be used to attempt suicide.

A typical brig day began with reveille at 0500 hours, followed by physical training consisting of running around a room a hundred times. Only five minutes were allowed for a breakfast of skimpy food such as a soup made from fish or cereal in small quantities. Prisoners were forced to run wherever they went. The day's activities consisted of some form of strenuous work, such as unloading sides of beef or heavy cement bags from a truck. Work was accompanied by harassment from the guards, who referred to their prisoners as brig rats. Typically, they also forced prisoners to shovel snow and then move it from one corner to another. Ten minutes were allowed for lunch before returning to their work detail. After a five-minute dinner break, work continued until 2300 hours when prisoners were returned to their cells. Prisoners slept on boards which were stacked outside to freeze during the day. No blankets were provided and cells were unheated—forcing the prisoners to huddle together for warmth. For punishment, guards filled a cell with water and removed bed boards so that prisoners couldn't rest on the floor. Suicides were common in some brigs, which led to speculation among sailors that some were actually murders committed by the guards.

In addition to the brig, the Soviet Navy was known to use disciplinary battalions to punish serious offenses such as striking an officer, murder, rape, or being AWOL for extended periods. Time served in these units was considered lost time by the navy, which would be made up through an extension of enlistment. Offenders who returned to duty from disciplinary battalions were often described as being cowered or broken. Their value afterwards to the navy was minimal, aside from being a warning to other sailors. For infractions concerning party discipline, the Communist Party itself handled these matters for such things as missing political meetings, or nonpolitical offenses such as drunkenness, theft, and going AWOL. Their punitive powers ranged from placing bad marks on a sailor's record to expulsion from the party. The KGB sometimes involved itself in the process of maintaining naval disciplinary matters. KGB officers in naval uniforms handled investigations related to mutinies, uprisings, and unit morale problems, and regular officers were usually afraid of them.

A Chance Informant:

*I*n April of 1985 imagine the surprise when someone from the CIA contacted our Soviet Embassy in Washington, D.C., and tried to sell us insider information. This also occurred during a few more insignificant meetings with this informant named Aldrich Ames, and while what he told us was known to be unimportant—we still paid him a great deal for it hoping he got hooked into supplying us with better information later on. And this is what eventually happened, but could we trust a person from the CIA offering us the names of their top spies living in our own country? Imagine how shocked we were when over the course of a few years, this informant divulged many important Soviet citizens who were spying for the West, including some of our own military officers, generals, a few colonels and even some KGB agents.

In total, nearly one-hundred important spies were compromised by him, with many being arrested and executed for treason against our motherland. The breadth of it all was great for us but must have shocked the CIA as well, since they never figured out our source of this information until after the Cold War was over. In some ways, though, it all came too late for us, in a few short years our country was broken up just like the spies that had been giving away many of our secrets.

1985 Akula Class

The last submarine design to be released by the Soviet Union before their collapse was the 4th generation Akula class SSN (*Project 971 Shchuka-B*). This was a nuclear-powered attack submarine built for strikes against naval carrier groups, and for patrolling in inner coastal regions. The 4th generation Akula class design was similar to the Victor-III and Sierra classes in that it had a distinctive bulb on top of the rudder that housed a sonar array. (See Figure 52.) They started entering service in 1985, and had a submerged speed of 35 knots. They had an overall length of 362 feet, and an operating depth limit of 1500 feet. For armament, each had four 21-inch torpedo tubes and four additional 25.6-inch torpedo tubes, all at the bow. They could carry a total of twelve super torpedoes such as the 65-76 version, and twenty-eight regular torpedoes, along with twelve tube launched weapons such as the SS-N-21 Sampson cruise missile. They were also capable of mine-laying. Each carried a crew of seventy-three. These were considered to be the quietest Soviet submarines ever built due to special construction techniques to limit noise generation. With additional improvements, they became the first stealth Soviet submarines that carried over to the Russian fleet. Only eight units were built before the Cold War ended.

The SS-N-21 Sampson (*S-10 Granat*) cruise missile used with the Akula class submarine was compatible with 21-inch torpedo tubes. With this system, accuracy to within 500 feet was possible. It had a maximum range of 1,300 nm at subsonic speeds up to 500 mph. The primary application for the SS-N-21 was as a submarine-launched weapon for nuclear strikes against theater targets, but also for initial strikes against targets in the continental United States. The Soviets later allocated SS-N-21s to the Sierra-II class, and also to the Victor-III class submarines. This weapon was meant to add considerable flexibility to the Soviet submarine force by carrying out nuclear missions, but was also meant to complicate Western defensive problems by converting an increasing number of Soviet submarines into land attack platforms.

Soviet Naval Spending:

The Soviet Navy's share of the defense budget in the latter years of the 1980s remained at around twenty percent of total spending, while overall spending was gradually being reduced. Even with significant spending being used for their construction programs for ships, including a variety of surface platforms ranging from small patrol craft to large cruisers, the lion's share of the construction budget continued to be devoted to the submarine program. The most notable trend over the final decade was an evolution towards what was called a balanced fleet–that is, a navy capable of fighting at both the nuclear and conventional levels, while still protecting state interests during peacetime.

In the early 1970s, the Soviet Navy could be described as a fleet with capabilities maximized for a short, intense war that rapidly escalated to the use of nuclear weapons. The small weapons loads and limited endurance of most surface combatants severely limited the Soviet Navy's ability for any sustained combat. In the mid-1970s, however, new classes of larger, more sophisticated ships with greater endurance, larger weapon loads, and extensive communication and electronic warfare systems began to enter service. This improved their capabilities for sustaining conventional combat and distant-area deployments.

In later years, the salient feature of the Soviet naval program was Moscow's emphasis on modernizing and upgrading their general purpose submarine force. Since 1978, general purpose submarine construction accounted for over three-fourths of the number of submarines being built, and about sixty percent of the total annual tonnage.

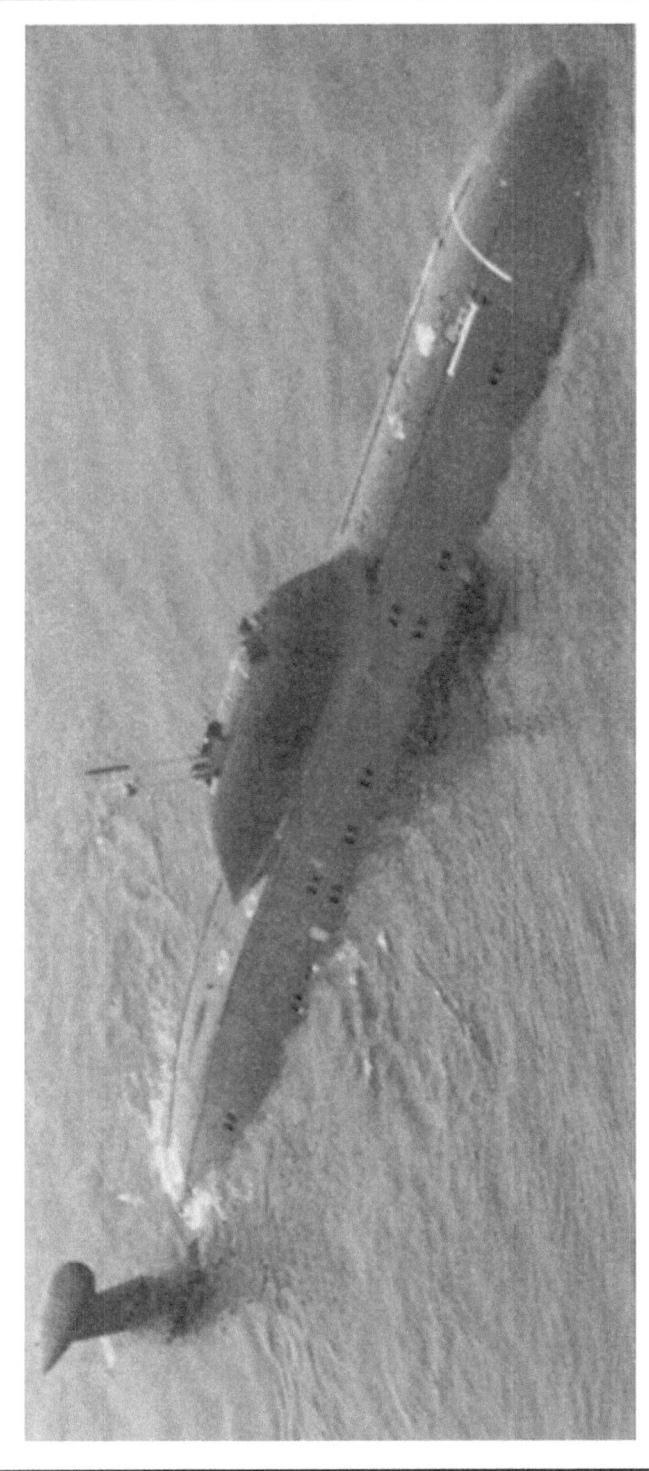

Figure 52. The Akula class nuclear-powered attack submarine was a 4th generation design, and was the final one to be released by the Soviet Union prior to their collapse. Only eight were completed before the Cold War ended.

The Soviets were still allocating considerable resources to their SSBN program. Initially, the construction rate of Yankee and Delta class SSBNs averaged about five per year and accounted for more than half of their Soviet nuclear submarine construction. Although construction rates tapered off and SSBN force levels stabilized to accommodate the levels agreed to in the SALT I Protocol (62 modern units and 950 launch tubes), the SSBN force still received significant emphasis, as evidenced by the construction of the new Delta-IV and Typhoon classes. (See Figure 53 on modern submarine production numbers.)

To avoid a reduction in the overall cruise missile force, the Akula class submarine was put into service with twelve land-attack cruise missiles launched from torpedo tubes, the SS-N-21. Eight of these were built until 1991. Another six submarines of the Oscar-II class went into service starting in 1986. Slightly larger than the Oscar-I class, these submarines were armed with twenty-four long-range anti-ship SS-N-19 cruise missiles. Yet another SSN, the Sierra-II class, designed to carry the SS-N-21 torpedo tube-launched cruise missile, also entered service. Meanwhile, the retrofitting of the SS-N-12 anti-ship cruise missile into Echo-IIs that began in the mid-1970s was nearly complete.

Eventually fourteen submarines were modified in this way, with three of those further upgraded to carry a newer version of the SS-N-12 cruise missile before the end of the Cold War. This robust general purpose submarine construction program had been driven primarily by Moscow's intention to close the technology gap between Soviet and Western submarines. Western advances in submarine noise reduction and sensor improvements raised uncertainties about the capabilities of much of their Soviet submarine force to carry out their wartime mission. Hence, since the introduction of the Victor-III class SSN in 1979, the Soviets steadily reduced the technology gap with their newest submarines.

	1975	1976	1977	1978	1979	1980	1981	1982	1983	1984	1985	1986	1987	1988	1989	1990	1991	Cumulative 1975-91
Total production																		
SSBNs																		
Delta-I	2	2	3															7
Delta-II	4																	4
Delta-III		4	2	2	2	2	1	1										14
Delta-IV										1	1	1	1	1	1	1		7
Typhoon							1	1	1	1			1		1			6
SSGNs																		
Charlie-II	1	1	1	1	1													5
Oscar-I Oscar-II						1			1			2	1	1	1	2		8
SSNs																		
Victor-II	1	1	1	2														5
Victor-III				2	4	4	3	2	3	2	1	2	1	1		2		25
Alfa			1	2	1	2												6
Mike									1									1
Sierra-I Sierra-II										1			1		1			3
Akula											1		1	2	1	2	1	8
SSs																		
Foxtrot	1	2	1		1	1	1	1	1									9
Kilo						1	1		3	3	1	2		3	1	5	2	22

Figure 53. A table showing Soviet submarine class production from 1975 to 1991.

Progress in Soviet submarine quieting, evidenced in the Oscar, Sierra, and Akula classes, including sonar and signal-processing improvements, all continued. While half of the Soviet nuclear attack force in the 1980s was composed of relatively quieter submarines, with the gap having nearly been closed when compared only to the Akula class, the US submarine fleet still enjoyed an overall acoustic advantage up until the end of the Cold War. Other factors behind the final decade of the Soviet submarine program included a deficiency in the number of submarines required to carry out the wide range of missions assigned to the force. For example, although the Northern and Pacific Fleets used about half of their available diesel-powered attack submarines to aid in nuclear ballistic sub defense, such units were less capable than SSNs which could operate in the under-ice environment increasingly used by Soviet SSBNs. In addition, about half of the Soviet submarine force was aging and was increasingly plagued with maintenance problems.

A Leaking Silo:

On October 3rd, 1986, our Yankee-I class nuclear submarine K-219 was on the thirtieth day of a routine patrol in the North Atlantic, in an area approximately one thousand kilometers east of the Bermuda Islands. At 0530 the submarine was transitioning from one depth to another when seawater began to enter the third missile silo on her port side, which caused explosive gases to form within the silo due to a fuel leak. The crew attempted to start a pump and open the hatch cover to vent the silo since the submarine had a previous accident with a leaking silo once before. This attempt at diffusing the danger ending up being too late. They found this out when a moment later a powerful explosion happened, the force of which blew upwards through the cover and ripped away portions of

the silo. Damage control quarters was quickly sounded–
and within a few moments–the submarine sank quickly
from a depth of forty meters down to three-hundred
meters.

A small fire that had broken out from the explosion was
extinguished, however dangerous gases started to fill
various compartments within the submarine. It crept
though the broken lines and filled passageways with an
orange haze that poisoned anyone who breathed it in. The
missile compartment was then evacuated, which left
crewmembers split between the forward and after
compartments. Frantic work continued to keep the
submarine from sinking further for many hours, until an
alarm signal was reported from the reactor room. The
damage was assessed and a determination was made that
the reactors needed to be shut down immediately due to
rising heat levels from a broken steam line and toxic gases.
Some within the crew were envisioning a nuclear core
explosion and resulting contamination of a Chernobyl-size
area if this was not accomplished rapidly. They attempted
a shutdown by using the emergency remote control system,
but it failed to work properly. Of those in the propulsion
area, only two crewmembers were knowledgeable enough
to go in and shut down the reactors manually. It was the
last resort and they had no other options at this point.

The first to go in was a senior lieutenant wearing
protective gear. He first obtained a special wrench and then
entered the reactor compartment. He knew the area like the
back of his hand, then found the first of four locations and
started turning the rod assembly. Even though he was
using a special wrench–it still took great strength to do it,
but at last it was completed just as the oxygen in his
breathing mask ran out. He stumbled out into the adjacent
compartment and collapsed from the heat and exertion
expended. Meanwhile the other seaman, a control-man,
was readied to enter with protective gear, and after they

had resuscitated the senior lieutenant and replaced his oxygen cartridge, they both went into the reactor room together to continue shutting down the cores. They found the second location and screwed the special wrench onto the nut, then started to turn the core. The extreme heat and gases though made it very tiring, and after resting between turns, they both worked together and eventually finished it. Two had now been turned fully. They moved over to the third location and again screwed on the special wrench, but not before they could start did the control-man collapse. The officer moved him away into a corner so he could try and recover, then went back and turned on the rod. When the third one was finally finished, the officer went back to the control-man and they both left the compartment together, where the officer collapsed into unconsciousness.

This left only the control-man to finish the job. He was given a fresh oxygen cartridge and a bottle of water, then he entered the reactor compartment again. All of this took time, and by now the temperature in the rod assembly area had risen to over 180 degrees Fahrenheit. Also great pressure was building, and despite all this, he managed to start screwing on the special wrench while having little strength left in his hands. Minutes went by for each turn as the heat and fumes took their toll on him. This went on for nearly an hour, but finally he finished the last rod. He had saved the remaining crew! He called the control room and they congratulated him for a job well done. Now he just had to leave the compartment. But he couldn't open the hatch because of the high pressure that had built up inside from the fumes, and even though he tried with all his strength, the hatch couldn't be budged. All attempts to equalize pressure between the compartments also failed. Attempts to break into the reactor compartment and save him also failed. The control-man was trapped. All they could hear was him tapping the bulkhead with a wrench for a short while, then without more oxygen—the taps eventually stopped. The nearby crew was forced to retreat into the ninth compartment to save themselves from the escaping heat and poisonous gases.

By this time at 2200 hours the crew in the forward compartments was still doing damage control to stop the flooding. But slowly they were losing the battle. These attempts to control the flooding and avoid sinking continued when Soviet ships arrived to help in a rescue, and with the reactor finally shut down it was now possible for the submarine to surface. Leaders in Moscow had informed Washington about this incident and declared that there was no chance of a nuclear explosion or accidental missile launch, even though such a chance had existed earlier. Then when submarine K-219 finally surfaced, the extent of the damage to the missile silo was evident. The explosion had torn its cover off and buckled steel was seen all around its perimeter. An eerie red color covered the metal surfaces around it like a bloody, open wound. An order was received that the disabled submarine should be towed back to base, and this was attempted by using a towline. However, all attempts at towing failed, just as the conditions inside the submarine were too dangerous to ignore. Then a fire broke out caused by a short circuit from one of the pumps. The crew was evacuated to the nearby Soviet ships, with the captain being the last to leave. At 1103 on October 6th, the submarine slipped under the surface and sank one last time, finally resting on the sea bottom at a depth of 5,500 meters.

When the crew returned to Moscow, they were expecting to be treated like heroes, but instead accusations about the possible causes of the accident were swirling. Did an American submarine, the USS Augusta, collide with K-219? Did any of our Soviet sailors sabotage our submarine while covertly being an enemy spy? Or was it simply a case of total incompetence? Even Gorbachev was asking many questions, and heads needed to roll. It was decided that the *captain was to be charged with sabotage, negligence, and treason for the loss of his submarine. Both he and the engineering head were also discharged from active military duty under Article 59e. The criminal case was eventually dismissed against the captain, who attempted an official appeal about his discharge. He was reminded to never raise the issue again. Lost in the drama of the time was how the seal on the silo had single-handedly caused the loss of our submarine–along with many of the crew.*

1990 Final Judgments:

The Soviet Navy's main role in military strategy wasn't changed substantially in the context of the Gorbachev revolution. The Navy had suffered cutbacks within defense spending, but radical changes to its missions or a major erosion in its combat capabilities never materialized as a result. Rather, from the mid-1980s, the Soviet Navy was still attempting further improvements in its war-fighting capabilities. They also were assuming greater responsibilities in a more unified military strategy, especially with enhanced roles in strategic strike operations and in national air defenses. This included a more integrated role for their general purpose submarine forces in theater warfare, and in the defense of their homeland. The Soviet Navy tried to absorb its lessened share through a combination of reduced operating tempo, cuts in personnel and accelerated retirements, with the scrapping of older ships and submarines, and through program cuts or slowdowns. Nevertheless, improvements were still underway through further development of improved surface ships, submarines, and naval aviation. Although the Navy had fewer ships and submarines in the fleet, the newer units were more capable, and submarines continued to enjoy a top priority.

Further refinements in the Soviet ballistic missile submarine force, particularly in terms of survivability, responsiveness, and the accuracy of sea-launched ballistic missiles, allowed their Soviet leadership a greater flexibility when deploying ballistic missile submarines. It also gave them a greater capability in using their submarines to conduct nuclear strikes against a broader range of targets. Soviet nuclear-armed sea-launched cruise missiles were primarily theater strike weapons. Although the Soviets considered countering Western ballistic missile submarines as their top naval priority, it was estimated that the Soviet Union's ability to detect and attack such submarines in the open ocean remained minimal up until the end of the Cold War.

The Soviets had actively pursued naval arms control initiatives in an effort to erode the US maritime advantage, including limitations on long-range cruise missiles, but this failed to ever materialize. Even with fewer general purpose naval units, the basic mission of the Soviet Navy never really changed at the end. It was still required to protect the USSR against any Western threats from the open sea. Only radical changes, such as decisions to eliminate the Navy's role in strategic strikes against the United States, its responsibilities for national air defense, or its support for operations on land, could produce a fundamental change in strategy. But such decisions were never made, or could have ever been accepted politically.

Beware The Ocean:

One of our experiments in Soviet development involved a single K-278 submarine of the Mike class ever being constructed, being a third generation nuclear attack submarine which evaluated fourth generation technologies, such as including an escape chamber. She was awarded the special name "Komsomolets" and had quickly set a record for submerged depth on her maiden voyage, diving to an incredible depth of just over one-thousand meters. One would think such a submarine to be almost unsinkable with such a rating, but as many have experienced throughout history, the ocean can sink the most seaworthy of vessels. And such a thing, although seemingly unthinkable, became a reality as she was out on her third patrol in the Barents Sea on April 7, 1989.

It all began at 1100 that morning while submerged at one-hundred and fifty meters, when the watch engineer noticed a problem in the seventh compartment. He called in the problem to control and was overtaken by the heat. The air temperature gauge showed it was over 160 degrees Fahrenheit in the compartment and rising! The captain sounded damage-control quarters, and as the ringing bells blared loudly, the crew scrambled to get to their stations within the submarine. Meanwhile, attempts were made to contact seventh compartment. No response! Then no response again! The decision was made to engage the fire-extinguishing system and flood the compartment with chemical gases, and it might have worked had an air-line not ruptured due to the fire. Instead, the fire grew stronger with every second that passed by. Next, the fire made its way into the sixth compartment, where it shut down a generator and made the reactor emergency system trip on. This effectively shut down any propulsion, so the submarine stopped moving forward, endangering all those aboard. At any moment, the submarine could sink like a rock to the bottom of the sea. Also unknown to the crew, carbon monoxide gas was being forced into the line that supplied air to the emergency breathing system for the crew. This was discovered after they began using it to stay at their stations, and some started passing out. Meanwhile, the reactor itself was completely shut down to prevent a nuclear accident.

The control room order was given for an emergency ballast blow, and this was carried out at the exact time it was needed. As it began working, the submarine slowly *started rising to the surface. What a miracle! With the smoke now arriving into the control room and visibility getting worse by the minute, the captain gave the order for all unnecessary personnel up to the bridge. As the submarine surfaced and the topside hatch was opened, they scrambled topside to safety. Inside a search was conducted in the fourth and fifth compartments to find out who was still there, and two crewmembers were found unconscious. These two were carried and taken topside with the others. After an emergency distress call was sent, radio contact was eventually made with an approaching Soviet aircraft above the horizon. Rescue would be directed to the area soon was the answer given. The pilot of the plane flew close to the submarine, and noticed the frothing of seawater back by the seventh compartment on the port side, with some smoke trailing in the wind behind her. This he reported back to base while continuing to circle in the area. After a few minutes the plane informed the captain aboard the sub that the earliest a ship could arrive at the site was at 1800. Even though this was still a few hours away, the captain and his crew were relieved at hearing the news. They still all expected a safe rescue and to be taken back to base. But after a brief time, this was not to be the case. One error made was safety equipment like wetsuits were not taken topside with them, and when the fire suddenly exploded out of control due to some leaking oxygen tanks feeding the flames, the submarine shuddered and began to sink.*

   "Rafts into the water" was the order given topside. The submarine's back deck was already underwater with the stern lapping under waves and disappearing. One sailor grabbed a raft and tried untying it, but no luck. Then another attempt, and it still couldn't be unfastened. Finally, a few more tries and it started floating away from the sub, then inflated upside down. The other raft was pulled away, and sent off. It also inflated upside down. The water was up over the feet of the survivors, who were now jumping into

the freezing water, and trying to swim for the rafts. In order to save anyone that might still be inside the sub, the decision was made to close the hatch, and this was done. Then the last of the seamen above jumped for the rafts as they felt the submarine disappear from beneath them. But the freezing water was so cold that they were already experiencing numbness in their limbs. "Swim, Swim." As they tried to cling to the two rafts, a few of the ones that were injured were told to climb on top of them. Others still floated beside them while trying to remain calm.

Inside the submarine, the experimental rescue chamber was the last hope for survival for five crew members. It was their last place to go just as the submarine started plunging to the bottom. They made it inside and dogged the hatch closed, then heard tapping sounds indicating someone was still wanting to enter. It was the engineering officer who had stayed behind to monitor the generators. All attempts to open the hatch failed, and those inside the chamber were left with no choice but to attempt detaching from the submarine without him. This proved unsuccessful until the instructions were followed again, and finally it happened at a depth of five-hundred meters. They had broken free! But the chamber proved not to be their total savior. When they finally hit the surface and the rescue hatch was opened, the pressure inside blew two of them out, with only one surviving, and the other three stayed inside helplessly as the chamber sank back to the bottom of the Barents Sea.

A Soviet plane still circled above the area and watched as the two rafts kept bobbing along in the waves below. The pilot could only witness the distress of the seamen on the surface as they waited for a rescue. Within an hour, many of the seamen were dying of hypothermia, and drifting away from the rafts. Others held onto the rope around the rafts with only their teeth, as their hands were frozen and useless. Then someone spotted a ship coming. They all sang out in hope. Twenty-seven ended up surviving the sinking and living to tell the story of the forty-two who had died that day under difficult circumstances and with unwavering bravery.

The Modernized SSBN Force:

One of the final ironies about the Cold War was that the Soviet Union finally achieved a modernized SSBN force made possible through further Typhoon and Delta-IV class submarines entering service just prior to their collapse. These Typhoon and Delta-IV class SSBNs had nearly replaced the earlier Yankee-I class submarine force. This resulted in a decrease in the total number of SSBN submarines, but maintained the same number of sea-based strategic warheads, since the earlier Yankee-I class had only sixteen warheads each, while each Typhoon class carried twenty SS-N-20 ballistic missiles, each armed with ten MIRV warheads—for a total of 200 warheads per submarine. This also resulted in a less vulnerable SSBN force since nearly all of these submarines could strike any distant targets in the United States from under the Arctic icecap or from their own home waters. In addition, these newer submarine designs were much quieter and harder to detect than the ones they had replaced.

The Soviet Union Ends:

The final collapse of our country really started in 1988 when Estonia declared their sovereignty from us, followed by Lithuania, along with Latvia. Things continued to deteriorate and on November 8th, 1989, parts of the Berlin Wall came down, which opened up the border between East and West Germany. Then three weeks later at the Malta Summit, our Soviet President Gorbachev and US President Bush both said that the Cold War was over, while some in *our country felt that such a declaration was still premature. However, more Soviet bloc countries declared their sovereignty from us over the following two years, and on Christmas Day in 1991, President Bush announced that America's confrontation with the Soviet Union was over, the nuclear threat, while far from gone, was receding. Eastern Europe was liberated and the Soviet Union existed no more. He claimed it was a major victory for both democracy and freedom. American–he said–had won the Cold War.*

Then a few days later the end of our country officially happened. We financially collapsed for many reasons, but the sacrifices of those who did all they could to win the Cold War wasn't done in vain, as it still lived on with our Russian people. The smaller military we inherited kept functioning, the economic sacrifices became even greater with us, but we grew stronger. The Cold War was over, but perhaps a new Cold War had begun. One that the West failed to recognize for many years until our war in Ukraine. One last important point to be made was our Soviet leadership never imagined the money would ever run out for us, but eventually it did. In America, the politicians still spend their money freely, and think as we did in the past that things will last forever. Could the United States itself ever collapse financially? Maybe the end result of all the combined spending was mutually assured destruction, but not in a nuclear sense. We only ended up spending each other into financial oblivion, but lived to see it through. Perhaps that was the safest ending we could have ever hoped for.

The Soviet Submarine Legacy:

The collapse of the Soviet Union officially came on December 26th, 1991, when the Soviet of Republics voted the Soviet Union out of existence. The Commonwealth of

Independent States, which had been formed only a few weeks earlier by signatures from Russia, Belarus and Ukraine, assumed control of the Soviet Armed Forces, while Russian President Boris Yeltsin took up residence at Gorbachev's former offices after he had resigned his position. It was both a blessing and a curse when Russia eventually received the majority of the former Soviet Navy from the commonwealth, including its entire nuclear submarine force, along with the various naval bases and related shore facilities. This was due to the fact that a substantial number of the nuclear submarines which they had acquired were in such bad disrepair that many were idled at their docks, while others were too dilapidated to ever sail again, but had been counted as operational to keep the allure of Admiral Gorshkov's Soviet fleet ambitions alive until the end. Some of the idled submarines needed air pumped inside them to remain afloat, while others had patches on their hulls to keep them from sinking.

While the Soviet Union may have recognized a need to reduce the active fleet in the past, they never had planned for an ending to the Cold War, nor the massive environmental crisis that ended up being created through the dismantling of their nuclear submarine program. The old ways of dumping low level radioactive waste into the ocean or sinking the submarines far away from shore could no longer be done since Russia would end up decommissioning nearly seventy-five percent of their inherited nuclear submarine fleet. The 3rd and 4th generation submarines were given the top priority to remain as a viable force, while the rest were left to be scrapped due to high operating costs, a lack of funding, and safety issues among other reasons. The majority of the Russian nuclear submarines remained based in the Northern Fleet, and this area is where local facilities were used to start the decommissioning process, including weapons removal, nuclear waste disposal, reactor core removal and rod storage, cutting up the submarines at drydock, and reactor compartment storage. The large quantities of metals recovered from salvage were valued at nothing more than scrap prices. This entire process took nearly twenty-five years to accomplish, with billions of dollars in funding coming from former adversaries as assistance.

Reflecting back on all four of the submarine phases during the Cold War, from 1950 until 1991 the Soviet Union produced a total of 698 submarines–464 of them were diesel-electric and 234 had nuclear propulsion–a total amount that was nearly triple of what was produced by the United States during the same timeframe. And of the 234 Soviet submarines with nuclear propulsion, about 180 of them ended up being decommissioned by the Russian government after the collapse of the USSR. What was once considered the mightiest submarine fleet in the world, the legacy Russian submarine fleet evolved into a much smaller and leaner force, yet even more potent. Instead of leading by sheer numbers, they now became quieter, carried more missiles and weapons, and were probably what Soviet Admiral Sergey Gorshkov had hoped to see during his lifetime. And while it came too late for his Soviet Union, the legacy of his fleet still lives on quietly under the oceans. Still operating for a day which we hope never happens.

The End

www.ingramcontent.com/pod-product-compliance
Lightning Source LLC
Chambersburg PA
CBHW020337010526
44119CB00001B/21